T0328595

Cambridge Elements ≡

Elements in Language Teaching
edited by
Heath Rose
Linacre College, University of Oxford
Jim McKinley
University College London

TASK-BASED LANGUAGE TEACHING

Daniel O. Jackson
Kanda University of International Studies

CAMBRIDGE
UNIVERSITY PRESS

Shaftesbury Road, Cambridge CB2 8EA, United Kingdom

One Liberty Plaza, 20th Floor, New York, NY 10006, USA

477 Williamstown Road, Port Melbourne, VIC 3207, Australia

314–321, 3rd Floor, Plot 3, Splendor Forum, Jasola District Centre,
New Delhi – 110025, India

103 Penang Road, #05–06/07, Visioncrest Commercial, Singapore 238467

Cambridge University Press is part of Cambridge University Press & Assessment,
a department of the University of Cambridge.

We share the University's mission to contribute to society through the pursuit of
education, learning and research at the highest international levels of excellence.

www.cambridge.org
Information on this title: www.cambridge.org/9781009068413

DOI: 10.1017/9781009067973

First published 2022

A catalogue record for this publication is available from the British Library.

ISBN 978-1-009-06841-3 Paperback
ISSN 2632-4415 (online)
ISSN 2632-4407 (print)

Task-Based Language Teaching

Elements in Language Teaching

DOI: 10.1017/9781009067973
First published online: September 2022

Daniel O. Jackson
Kanda University of International Studies
Author for correspondence: Daniel O. Jackson, Jackson-d@kanda.kuis.ac.jp

Abstract: This Element is a guide to task-based language teaching (TBLT), for language instructors, teacher educators, and other interested parties. The Element first provides clear definitions and principles related to communication task design. It then explains how tasks can inform all stages of curriculum development. Diverse, localized cases demonstrate the scope of task-based approaches. Recent research illustrates the impact of task design (complexity and mode) and task implementation (preparation, interaction, and repetition) on various second-language outcomes. The Element also describes particular challenges and opportunities for teachers using tasks. The epilogue considers the potential of TBLT to transform classrooms, institutions, and society.

This Element also has a video abstract: www.cambridge.org/dojackson

Keywords: pedagogic task design, curriculum development, language education, classroom research, teacher education

ISBNs: 9781009068413 (PB), 9781009067973 (OC)
ISSNs: 2632-4415 (online), 2632-4407 (print)

Contents

1 What Is TBLT?

1.1 A Framework for Language Teaching

As an approach to communicative language teaching, task-based language teaching (TBLT) originated in the mid-1980s. It has grown to become one of the most widely recognized options for designing and implementing language instruction today. As a field of academic inquiry, TBLT has achieved a number of milestones, including the inauguration of the International Conference on TBLT in 2005, since organized every two years under the auspices of the International Association for Task-Based Language Teaching (IATBLT), a book series published by John Benjamins since 2009, and the launch of *TASK: Journal on Task-Based Language Teaching and Learning* in 2021. In terms of its implementation, TBLT has matured from an alternative approach to a mainstream educational policy initiative encouraged or adopted in schools in Belgium, Hong Kong, and New Zealand, among other regions. Increasingly, it is offered as a subject in language teacher education programs, featured at teaching conferences and in professional workshops, and is carried out by teachers with students, during face-to-face or online lessons.

Thus, TBLT is a way of teaching languages and a robust area of inquiry. In practice, language educators around the world use tasks to coherently frame their teaching. This coherence can be seen from various perspectives. First, 'task' provides a useful concept for framing the reasons *why* languages are taught, *what* to teach (the particular content), and *how* to teach (the classroom procedures). Second, in a practical sense, the literature on TBLT offers guidance on using the concept of task to link elements of curriculum design such as materials, teaching, and testing. Lastly, and most importantly, TBLT epitomizes the notion that classroom instruction should be responsive to learners' needs for using language in the real world.

Tasks enable learners to acquire communicative abilities and to participate in social activities relevant to their present or future goals. There has been much discussion and debate regarding the proposal that real-world tasks should form the basis of language teaching, beginning with Long (1985). The appeal of TBLT is that it seeks to identify and utilize activities valued by learners as the impetus for curriculum development. How the use of tasks facilitates acquisition of language and fosters participation in society is a matter of considerable theoretical and practical interest. It furthermore involves reconsideration of the teacher's role, which in TBLT contrasts with traditional educational practices. According to Long and Ahmadian (2022, pp. xxvi–xxvii), TBLT is growing in popularity because it is:

1. perceived by adult learners as clearly designed with their specific needs in mind;
2. preferred by students and teachers to traditional approaches to language teaching;
3. supported by evidence from comparison studies, which demonstrate its benefits over traditional approaches to language teaching;
4. compatible with other contemporary approaches, such as bilingual education, content-and-language-integrated learning, and English medium instruction;
5. consistent with findings from second language acquisition research on linguistic development and learner factors.

1.2 The Aim and Organization of This Element

It is relevant here to briefly note my background within the TBLT community, as well as my approach and aim. I earned my MS in Education at the University of Pennsylvania, where I first encountered the notion of tasks in language teaching in the late Teresa Pica's stimulating classes and seminal publications. Upon graduating, I served in the English Language Program at J. F. Oberlin University, where I often employed tasks in teaching and assessment. Later, as I completed my PhD in Second Language Studies at the University of Hawai'i at Mānoa, I had the honor of studying with John Norris, Lourdes Ortega, and Peter Robinson, whose important contributions to TBLT are described in this Element. In my research, I adopt a cognitive-interactionist stance on language learning that emphasizes tasks as a valuable means of providing learners with opportunities for input, output, and feedback. I have also advocated a range of theoretical views on tasks in classroom research (Jackson & Burch, 2017) and conducted studies on preservice teacher psychology within tasks (Jackson, 2021; Jackson & Shirakawa, 2020). In my current role as a professor in the English Department and the MA TESOL Program at Kanda University of International Studies, I have found that, although excellent, authoritative accounts of TBLT have been published (e.g., Ellis et al., 2019; Long & Ahmadian, 2022; Van den Branden, 2022), the need exists for a short, practical guide to the main concepts and issues in task-based language education. My aim is to make this field accessible to a wider audience of teachers.

As just noted, this Element offers a concise guide to the main concepts and issues in TBLT. It can be used by teachers individually or in groups, perhaps as a resource in preservice or in-service teacher education courses and workshops.

The present introductory section orients readers to TBLT and provides key definitions and examples, as well as offering commentary on communication task design. Section 2 guides readers through the familiar elements of a language curriculum (needs analysis, sequencing of content, materials development, teaching, testing, and evaluation) to illustrate how each can be informed by tasks. Section 3 then adopts a case study approach to demonstrate how teachers of diverse languages have found TBLT useful in their particular contexts. The longest section of the Element is Section 4, which presents a review of recent empirical studies divided into two distinct aspects that concern practitioners: task design (i.e., complexity and modality) and task implementation (i.e., preparation, interaction, and repetition). Section 5 then provides an overview of some of the central issues faced by teachers in understanding and using tasks. In the epilogue in Section 6, I offer a brief critique of the potential of TBLT to bring about positive change in classrooms, institutions, and societies. The Element concludes with an appendix of questions designed to facilitate discussion after each of the aforementioned sections has been read.

Why use tasks in the first place? There are many answers, which will become apparent throughout this text. In this opening section, the following rationales will be presented. In short, among the clearest benefits of using tasks are that they can be designed to offer students:

- opportunities for meaningful communication in their second language (L2), which can lead to the acquisition of new language through comprehensible input, feedback, and modified output;
- practice to attain fluency and utilize specific features of language that may be challenging to learn;
- choices regarding lesson content and procedures and thus more meaningful and engaging learning experiences.

As described in this section, tasks are compatible with a wide range of teaching approaches. Subsequently, from Section 2 onwards, further advantages gained from entirely task-based approaches will be considered.

1.3 Definitions

There is a difference between *target tasks*, or real-world activities learners ultimately aim to accomplish in their target language, and *pedagogic tasks*, which are instructional activities derived from target tasks. During engagement in pedagogic tasks, learners "use language, with an emphasis on meaning, to attain an objective" (Bygate, Skehan, & Swain, 2001, p. 11). This basic definition incorporates many others that have been offered over the years. According to it, the following practices would not fittingly be described as tasks: (1) learning about the target language without actually using it, such as when listening to an explanation of it in one's first language; (2) using the language mechanically rather than meaningfully, as in the memorized dialogues or choral repetition associated with the audio-lingual method; and (3) using language meaningfully but without any overt goal, as in free conversation. Of course, one might benefit minimally from such activities, but they also illustrate an essential categorical distinction.

Besides the disregard for learners' needs in these examples of what is *not* a task, it is worth briefly considering how each of Bygate and colleagues' criteria is compatible with recent assumptions regarding learning and language. Namely, the specification that tasks must involve language use acknowledges that learning accrues gradually through practice in comprehending and producing oral and written discourse. The prioritization of meaning is supported by various functional theories of language, which view it as a tool for communication. Lastly, establishing objectives helps fuel learner engagement and clarify expected outcomes. A wide range of theoretical support for TBLT, often sharing an emphasis on learning by doing, has been described elsewhere (see Ahmadian & García Mayo, 2018; East, 2021; Ellis et al., 2019; Jackson & Burch, 2017; Long, 2015; Norris, 2009; Samuda & Bygate, 2008).

Moving from theory to practice, a crucial aspect of using tasks involves the difference between the *task-as-workplan* and the *task-in-process* (Breen, 1987). Importantly, the design of a task can predict neither entirely how it should be implemented for a given group of learners nor its outcomes. The original plan for the task, including its stated objective and procedures, unfolds according to the teacher's implementation and learner responses. The potential of the task to shape learning emerges from psycholinguistic and social activity during this task-in-process. The terms *retask* and *detask* (Samuda, 2015) have been used to refer to how teachers, as well as students, may alter plans during instruction. Further useful distinctions include those between *written* versus *oral* tasks, as well as *monologic* (narrative) versus *dialogic* (interactive) tasks. The examples in Section 1.4 are oral, dialogic tasks.

1.4 Task Types

How can education be linked to relevant, real-world activities while also promoting meaningful language use with a clear objective in sight? For instance, having determined through personal observation and consultation with colleagues that a group of young learners would value the ability to sing popular songs in their L2, a teacher might consider how this target task could be modified for them in a way that fosters learning through interaction. One possibility is to distribute two sets of lyrics for a given song wherein missing words in each set are present in the other, have the students exchange information verbally to complete the lyrics, and then practice singing the song together. In this example, the underlying task type is called a jigsaw task. Pedagogic *task types* are accounts of classroom tasks in terms of abstract categories (e.g., Pica, Kanagy, & Falodun, 1993; Prabhu, 1987; Robinson, 2001; Skehan, 1996; Willis, 1996). Typological descriptions are helpful to researchers, designers, and teachers because they may be used to classify tasks, discern their similarities and differences, and rank them according to their learning potential, among other uses.

This section offers examples of each type of task in the typology put forth by Pica, Kanagy, and Falodun (1993). Being one of several possible choices, this typology was selected for the following reasons. First, Pica and colleagues covered five pedagogic task types, thereby incorporating earlier discussions that are helpful but made fewer distinctions (e.g., Prabhu, 1987). Second, rather than mainly describing the activity associated with tasks (e.g., Willis, 1996), their stated purpose was to present a "typology which can be used to differentiate tasks according to their contributions to language learning" (Pica, Kanagy, & Falodun, 1993, p. 10), for both teachers and researchers. Third, related to this goal, even though recent frameworks offer more fine-grained detail regarding the psycholinguistic demands of tasks and are augmented by task sequencing principles (e.g., Robinson, 2015), Pica and colleagues' application of their typology to previously published teaching and research materials demonstrates its feasibility for designing, modifying, or understanding a wide range of materials. It is therefore a good starting point for understanding how task design may contribute to providing comprehensible input, negative feedback, and opportunities for modified output during learner–learner interaction.

Table 1 summarizes the descriptions in Sections 1.4.1–1.4.5 and illustrates how the five task types differ by interactional activity (i.e., information flow and interaction requirement) and communication goal (i.e., goal orientation and outcome options). To briefly gloss the table headers, information flow concerns whether there is only one speaker or more than one speaker (1 vs. 2 way). Interaction requirement refers to whether it is necessary or optional (+/- Required) for learners to interact. Goal orientation describes whether the task orients learners to the same goal or not (+/- Convergent). Lastly, outcome options include a single, fixed outcome (e.g., a math problem), a single, variable outcome (e.g., an election), or can be nonspecific.

Table 1 Pedagogic task types (adapted from Pica, Kanagy, & Falodun, 1993)

Type	Information flow	Interaction requirement	Goal orientation	Outcome options
Jigsaw	2 way	+ Required	+ Convergent	1 fixed
Information gap	1 or 2 way	+ Required	+ Convergent	1 fixed
Problem-solving	2 or 1 way	- Required	+ Convergent	1 fixed
Decision-making	2 or 1 way	- Required	+ Convergent	1 variable
Opinion exchange	2 or 1 way	- Required	- Convergent	Any or none

The following subsections present and discuss examples of each type. As described later (Section 2.1), TBLT is based on needs. This point is demonstrated by using the running example of nutrition, although TBLT, like most education, often caters to less basic and more psychological needs. All five examples form a unit of lessons for US-based adult learners whose needs include understanding English concerning proper nutrition. Specifically, they aim to support learners' ability to understand the nutritional value of food, make healthy choices, share preferences, and so on. Each subsection provides a brief definition, followed by the sample task, and a discussion of its potential for classroom language acquisition, based on Pica, Kanagy, and Falodun's (1993) study. Though the examples describe pair work, these task types can also be the foundation for group work.

1.4.1 Jigsaw

In a jigsaw task, learners engage in a two-way exchange of information. The exchange leads to completing some type of puzzle, hence the name. In the jigsaw and information gap tasks (see Section 1.4.2), interlocutors have clearly defined roles as information provider and/or information requester. In the case of the jigsaw task, both roles are held by each speaker. Because they each have only a portion of the information needed, they must take turns to gather all of it. The example here unfolds in two stages, which are called the input stage and communication stage (Anderson, 2019). During the input stage, the teacher gives pairs of students two different nutrition facts labels for sandwich bread (see Figure 1), asking them not to show their information to their partner. The teacher then asks the students to read their labels silently and checks understanding of the language with the whole class. As soon as they are ready to begin the communication stage, the students cooperate to find out which product is more nutritious and why (i.e., it has more fiber, protein, and vitamins and less

White			Wheat		
Nutrition Facts			**Nutrition Facts**		
14 servings per container			14 servings per container		
Serving size	1 slice (50g)		**Serving size**	1 slice (50g)	
Amount per serving			Amount per serving		
Calories	**130**		**Calories**	**130**	
	% Daily value			% Daily value	
Total Fat 1g		1%	**Total Fat** 1.5g		2%
Saturated Fat 0g		0%	Saturated Fat 0g		0%
Trans Fat 0g			*Trans* Fat 0g		
Cholesterol 0mg		0%	**Cholesterol** 0mg		0%
Sodium 230mg		10%	**Sodium** 120mg		5%
Total Carbohydrate 26g		9%	**Total Carbohydrate** 26g		9%
Dietary Fiber 1g		4%	Dietary Fiber 4g		14%
Total Sugars 4g			Total Sugars 4g		
Includes 4g Added Sugars		8%	Includes 4g Added Sugars		8%
Protein 4g			**Protein** 6g		
Vitamin D 0mcg		0%	Vitamin D 0mcg		0%
Calcium 30mg		2%	Calcium 50mg		4%
Iron 1mg		6%	Iron 1.8mg		10%
Potassium 50mg		0%	Potassium 125mg		2%

Figure 1 Two nutrition facts labels: white versus wheat bread (amounts are a composite based on actual products)

fat, sodium, and sugar). To reach this conclusion, the learners verbally share their information.

The main advantage of the jigsaw task derives from the need for both participants to interact in order to converge on one solution. To compare all of the data, participants must sustain their interaction over multiple turns, incorporating lexical items that may be new or unfamiliar. They may also engage in further discussion to weigh the importance of any differences uncovered. For these reasons, Pica, Kanagy, and Falodun (1993, p. 21) claimed the jigsaw to be, "the type of task most likely to generate opportunities for interactants to work toward comprehension, feedback, and interlanguage modification processes related to successful SLA [second language acquisition]." This claim has been supported by face-to-face studies as well as those involving text-based computer-mediated communication (Blake, 2000).

1.4.2 Information Gap

Like jigsaw tasks, information gap tasks also require messages to be exchanged. However, they need only involve a one-way exchange: one person requests the information while the other provides it. A two-way exchange can happen if the listener actively seeks confirmation of the information received, or if the listener and speaker alternate roles. The goal of each person in the interaction is the same (+ Convergent) and there is one fixed outcome according to the input provided. As an example, the teacher could first have students write down their favorite recipe. This can follow a simple formula: the name and origin of the dish, the ingredients, and a list of steps. Once this material has been prepared, the first student in the pair describes their recipe to a partner, who takes notes. Then, they switch roles and repeat the task. Having students write down each other's recipes would benefit their interaction, as that can prompt them to seek clarification and confirmation. Doing so would also allow the students and teacher to check the accuracy of the exchange.

Alternatively, if the teacher rather than the students prepares the input, it is possible to design information gap tasks drawing attention to specific language features that are difficult to acquire due to low salience. Research on such tasks by Pica, Kang, and Sauro (2006) found a strong association between inter-actional processes and the noticing of specifically targeted forms. For example, while working in pairs to complete tasks requiring them to discuss and make choices about English articles, pronouns, determiners, and verb morphology, intermediate-level learners' interactions often showed evidence of noticing these targeted forms. In Schmidt's (1990) account, noticing, or conscious registration of language, is necessary for the acquisition of an L2. Although many tasks do not require such close attention to language input, Pica and colleagues assumed on the basis of their evidence that task-based interaction can prompt learners to notice. Maps, drawings, texts, and other materials can provide content for information gap tasks.

1.4.3 Problem-Solving

In a problem-solving task, learners are expected to interact to find a single solution to a given problem. As an example, consider a lesson where the teacher asks students to sit in pairs. The task input (Figure 2) is then displayed to the whole class. The teacher explains that these items are all popular snack foods, which differ in their calorie content, then instructs the students in pairs to discuss each example with the goal of ranking them from the least to most calories. The outcome of these discussions can be checked easily by having a student or students write the answer on the chalkboard: carrot < apple < banana < frozen yogurt < croissant < pizza slice. Then, any discrepancies in the ranking among pairs can be dealt with and follow-up discussions on the topic can be conducted.

Pica, Kanagy, and Faldoun (1993) noted some problems with problem-solving tasks. Namely, as seen in Table 1, the information should flow in two

Figure 2 Popular snack foods

directions, but if either student does not possess the requisite confidence, knowledge, or skill, then the other may lead throughout the discussion. Because the information requester versus provider roles are unspecified, the design does not strictly require interaction. These problems also apply to decision-making and opinion exchange tasks (see Sections 1.4.4 and 1.4.5). In the example, it may turn out that only one individual dominates the discussion. To promote more equal participation, the teacher might instruct students to take turns giving their answers and provide reasons for them. However, the fact remains that the amount and quality of interaction may be limited in comparison to jigsaw tasks, in which the discourse is more predictable. On the other hand, this design, like the previous two, has an advantage because its shared, fixed goal provides a clear direction and endpoint for the discussion.

1.4.4 Decision-Making

The decision-making task encourages learners to discuss a given topic and agree upon one of a finite number of acceptable outcomes. Other possible outcomes suggested by the input may be unacceptable. To illustrate, the teacher could provide the class with copies of a restaurant menu (Figure 3) to read. The task involves a scenario in which students are at lunch with a friend who needs assistance to understand the menu. This friend would prefer a meal that contains protein and vegetables, but no dairy. The teacher asks pairs of students to look over the menu in order to help choose a suitable option. Based on the criteria

---

Menu

BAKED MACARONI & CHEESE *served with garden salad*.................14

SMOKED CHICKEN *served with mashed potatoes & string beans*......22

CHEESEBURGER *on a toasted bun served with French fries*.............20

GRILLED SALMON *served with brown rice & steamed carrots*............24

GARDEN SALAD *with fresh lettuce, tomatoes, & cucumber*..............10

Figure 3 Menu

provided, two menu options can be eliminated immediately (those containing cheese) and a third (the salad) would not satisfy the need for protein. This leaves two choices, either of which constitutes an acceptable suggestion. The students agree on one of these and explain their choice to the class.

As already noted, the interactional activity in decision-making tasks is the same as in problem-solving tasks. The information on which the decision is based is shared among the students, who are expected to talk in order to reach a common goal, though there is no built-in requirement to interact. The distinguishing feature of this task is that while it requires an outcome, that outcome may vary (Pica, Kanagy, & Falodun, 1993). This brief example leaves room for only two options, but more could be added by increasing the number of items on the menu. Indeed, doing so might lead to more substantial discussion. Samuda and Bygate (2008) presented a task they called 'Things in Pockets,' in which students given a number of objects found in someone's coat pockets are asked to reach a consensus on the owner's identity. These authors made the point that the discourse emerging from such tasks has important qualities such as the potential for social engagement and collaborative thinking.

1.4.5 Opinion Exchange

In an opinion exchange task, learners are expected to share their opinions in order to discuss or debate a topic. Continuing with the diet and nutrition theme, the instructor could pair students up to have them discuss which locally produced foods they enjoy eating. Based on Pica, Kanagy, and Falodun's (1993) study (see Table 1 of this Element), the flow of information would presumably be two-way, but if either student is unfamiliar with the food sourced locally, then it will become one-way. Interaction is possible, but not required. The communication goal of opinion exchange tasks poses unique challenges. This design does not provide an inherent goal for the discussion to converge on. If students express disagreement, their goal orientation would be considered divergent. Besides, the goal is relatively simple: state any local food product or combination thereof, or none at all. For all of these reasons, exchanging opinions is unlikely to guarantee learners equal opportunities for conversational interaction to the extent seen in jigsaw and information gap tasks. Nonetheless, opinion exchange would be appropriate for different aspects of L2 development (Skehan, 1998). In fact, divergent tasks, in which learners produce additional clauses to support their arguments, have been shown to generate more syntactically complex discourse than convergent ones, in face-to-face (Duff, 1986) and computer-mediated (Jackson, 2011) settings. To communicate effectively in an L2, one must share opinions. Tasks that promote this ability also provide valuable opportunities for students to raise issues or concerns that might not otherwise come to light.

1.5 Additional Perspectives on Task Design

The previous section focused on how task design may shape classroom discourse to bring about favorable conditions for L2 acquisition (i.e., comprehensible input, negative feedback, and opportunities for modified output). Before going further, it is worth briefly noting two additional perspectives on the design of tasks. These views lead to broader understandings of the value of tasks in language education.

First, learning opportunities in TBLT have been viewed in terms of the task-essentialness (Loschky & Bley-Vroman, 1993; Ortega, 2007) of certain language items, which may be challenging to acquire under more naturalistic learning conditions. According to this perspective, tasks vary in terms of whether they make the comprehension or production of specific grammatical constructions essential, useful, or natural. It is easier to design one-way tasks that make comprehension of certain features essential to successful performance, although two-way tasks, such as those just described, can also be evaluated in terms of the essentialness of language features. As for grammar, in the problem-solving task (Section 1.4.3), comparatives are highly useful (e.g., *carrots have fewer calories than apples, frozen yogurt has more calories than a banana*). The concept of essentialness has also been extended to pronunciation (Solon, Long, & Gurzynski-Weiss, 2017). The jigsaw task in Section 1.4.1 makes the use of the schwa essential because this sound occurs in several words (e.g., *sodium, calcium, potassium*) that learners can be expected to use. Teachers might leverage these opportunities to draw attention to language, or promote increased fluency.

Second, more recently, the learners' level of engagement has been recognized as a major consideration in task-based learning. Philp and Duchesne (2016) described engagement in terms of its cognitive (e.g., attention), behavioral (e.g., time on task), social (e.g., affiliation), and emotional (e.g., feelings) facets. Researchers have measured engagement in various ways. With regard to task design, findings suggest that key dimensions of engagement are enhanced when using learner-generated as opposed to teacher-generated content (Lambert, Philp, & Nakamura, 2017; Phung, Nakamura, & Reinders, 2021). In other words, giving learners some control over the content appears to make tasks more meaningful and engaging. Among the examples provided, the information gap task in Section 1.4.2 does this by inviting learners to exchange their favorite recipes. It is sometimes easy to make minor adjustments to existing tasks in order to allow creativity and promote engagement. For example, the decision-making task (Section 1.4.4) could be redesigned so that learners first write down menu items individually, pool them to create their own menu, and then discuss which ones would make appropriate choices based on certain dietary restrictions.

These views are helpful for understanding the value of tasks, though in a broader sense, TBLT offers even more than conversational interaction, language practice, and learner engagement. As the following sections demonstrate, the outcomes can extend far beyond even these important goals.

2 The Task-Based Curriculum

Tasks are the building blocks for the development of task-based language curricula.[1] The components that define a curriculum and its development include needs analysis, objectives, testing, materials, and teaching, as well as ongoing evaluation of each of these elements (Brown, 1995). The design of task-based curricula (Long, 2015; Long & Norris, 2000; Norris, 2009) is similar, albeit distinguished by a focus on tasks at each stage. In terms of the learner's contribution, strictly task-based syllabi differ from those of traditional language teaching because they are *analytic*, rather than synthetic (Wilkins, 1976, as cited in Long & Crookes, 1992). That is, students *analyze* and perform tasks under the assumption that they will use their own abilities and knowledge to learn new, developmentally appropriate language, instead of being taught from a prescribed list of disconnected grammatical structures, presented piece-by-piece, which they must themselves recombine for use in later communication. To supplement learners' own analysis of the language used in tasks,

---

[1] As a reviewer helpfully pointed out, 'curriculum' has the same meaning as 'syllabus' in some parts of the world.

teachers can provide a focus on form. As described by Long and Robinson (1998), focus on form involves a momentary shift of attention (via recasts, clarification requests, and so on) to learner language produced during task performance. Another way in which task-based curricula potentially differ from traditional approaches is that learners are given a wider range of options for negotiating content and procedures (Breen & Littlejohn, 2000).

The view of tasks outlined in the preceding paragraph has aptly been described as uppercase Task-Based Language Teaching by Long (2015). Contrary to this scenario, it should be noted that, in practice, tasks are often viewed as "simply a context for learners to experience language in a range of ways" (Bygate, 2000, p. 188). Indeed, the acronym TBLT may be adopted as an umbrella term for any use of tasks in language teaching. Fully task-based programs are outnumbered by task-supported implementations, which put less emphasis on the overall role of tasks. Given that hybrid or task-supported options are described elsewhere (e.g., Ellis, 2018; Samuda & Bygate, 2008), this section will focus on the practicalities of orienting to tasks at each stage in a language curriculum, as in an uppercase or strong version of TBLT. The perspective offered here acknowledges that without a commitment to the coherent integration of tasks throughout programs, the maximal effectiveness of TBLT cannot properly be evaluated (Norris, 2009).

2.1 Needs Analysis

Needs analysis is the process of identifying the needs that a given learner group aims to fulfill through their education. The assumption is that it is more efficient, particularly in the case of adults, to tailor instruction to the specific academic, professional, or vocational domain in which the learners intend to use language. Language curriculum developers who undertake needs analyses utilize a wide range of sources (e.g., literature reviews, learners, and experts) and methods (e.g., interviews, questionnaires, and observations) (Long, 2005). Long argued that adopting tasks as the focal point avoids a bottleneck in such analyses. Experts typically possess considerable knowledge regarding their professional domains, but are untrained in linguistic description. This situation makes it challenging for curriculum designers to filter out relevant language from the wealth of information domain experts can provide. Ultimately, the needs analysis should accurately reflect the domain and spotlight how language is used within it. Therefore, collaboration between outside experts and applied linguists is recommended to provide valid and useful information about both the content and the language taught and assessed throughout the curriculum (Long, 2015).

Several examples of needs analyses illustrate its potential to foster TBLT. First, Park (2015) examined the needs of English as a foreign language (EFL) students in an urban middle school in Korea. The sources included students, teachers, and relevant documents. Descriptive analyses of survey data indicated students' perceived needs and their preferences regarding participation styles, learning strategies, and conversation topics, which were compared with teacher results to identify areas of agreement and disagreement. Both groups valued preparation for examinations, as well as communication, which has implications for implementing tasks in this context.

Second, Malicka, Gilabert Guerrero, and Norris (2019) conducted a study with hotel receptionists in Barcelona, Spain, including both experts (those with three to five years' work experience) and novices (tourism students interning at hotels). Based on interviews and on-site observations, they identified a variety of *target task types* (e.g., greeting and saying farewell to clients, providing directions, and solving problems) and their frequency. The interviewees were also asked to assess the relative ease/difficulty of the tasks. These results were used to design a task-based unit on handling overbooking, which was perceived as a difficult task, comprising simple, complex, and +complex task versions.

Third, Oliver (2020) documented the needs of Aboriginal students at a vocational high school in Western Australia. Various sources were used, including classroom observations and student, as well as teacher, interviews. Examination of these sources revealed that school teachers focused on meeting students' needs related to occupational, social, and life skills. The author describes how these needs were met through authentic, culturally appropriate tasks. Other recent examples have focused on the language needs of medical students using isiZulu (Gokool & Visser, 2021) and Syrian refugee parents using Turkish (Toker & Sağıç, 2022).

Needs analysis is one of the features distinguishing a strong version of TBLT from its weaker variants. Indeed, considering that L2 learning can be a choice or a necessity, some argue that general approaches to curriculum development, as often seen in commercial English as a second language (ESL) and EFL textbooks, are "particularly detrimental" (Serafini, 2022, p. 75) when learners need assistance in integrating into society. The nature and scope of learner needs are highly differentiated, as these three studies illustrate. In Park's study, they included academic and social needs, in Malicka's study, they involved highly specific occupational duties, and in Oliver's study, they encompassed workplace and social skills. Detailed knowledge of the sectors relevant to learners' future success is the first step in selecting and sequencing appropriate tasks for instruction.

2.2 Task Selection and Sequencing

Assuming the needs analysis has provided detailed information about the target tasks, these can be reclassified into more general target task types from which pedagogic tasks can be derived to create a syllabus (Long & Norris, 2000; Long, 2015). To return to the aforementioned study by Malicka, Gilabert Guerrero, and Norris (2019), 'overbooking', a challenging target task that hotel employees sometimes faced, was classified under the target task type 'solving problems'. This selection process led to the development of three, increasingly more complex pedagogic tasks. Each of these involved having learners, playing the role of a receptionist at a popular hotel, leave a voice message with various clients concerning their reservation details and room options. These steps are meant to transform real-world, target tasks into more accessible, instructional tasks that are useful to teachers and learners.

In the case of Park's (2015) research in the Korean middle school EFL setting (also reviewed in Section 2.1), the author noted broad agreement between students, teachers, and the national curriculum in terms of the need to develop communicative skills. A key suggestion here was to develop instruction based on target tasks which participants had identified, including sending email, traveling in English-speaking countries, giving directions to visitors to Korea, playing online games with an English speaker, and volunteering for community service overseas. Though this study did not seek to develop pedagogic tasks, it did provide highly valuable information for those responsible for doing so. In Section 2.3, materials development based on such advice is dealt with in detail.

Sequencing means to arrange these pedagogic tasks in a principled order on the syllabus. In keeping with the overall approach, it is determined by nonlinguistic criteria. One proposal is that cognitive complexity should be used as the basis of sequencing (Robinson, 2007, 2011a, 2011b, 2015; see especially Baralt, Gilabert, & Robinson, 2014). As for the effect of sequencing on language production, studies comparing repeated performance on simple versus complex tasks have shown small, yet meaningful, effects on learner production in terms of accuracy and fluency, though not syntactic complexity (Jackson & Suethanapornkul, 2013). Surprisingly, it appears difficult to empirically demonstrate that a sequence of simple to complex tasks yields better results than a random sequence across groups of learners. Malicka (2014) addressed this issue using two sequencing orders: (1) simple to complex versus (2) randomized sequencing. Learners in these two groups performed three tasks involving hotel clients and their complexity, accuracy, and fluency were measured. Task complexity influenced oral production in each of these dimensions. As expected, on complex tasks, fluency decreased whereas accuracy and syntactic complexity increased. However, the sequencing did not influence results: no differences were found across the two groups. Similarly, Gilabert and Barón (2018) grouped learners into (1) simple to complex versus (2) randomized sequence conditions, within which they carried out four email writing tasks. In this case, ten experts rated the learners' pragmatic performance holistically. No group differences were reported based on this measure. So, the effect of sequencing oral or written tasks specifically according to increasing cognitive complexity is an area where more research is needed (see Sasayama, Malicka, & Norris, in press, cited in Sasayama & Norris, 2019).

Pending further evidence, other criteria that may offer answers to the problem of sequencing tasks include: the importance or urgency of the target task to learners, how often it is expected to occur, and whether is it ordinarily encountered as part of a sequence (e.g., applying for a job, attending an interview, accepting an offer by email). Another intriguing possibility is to allow learners choice with regard to the order in which they complete certain tasks (Candlin, 1987).

2.3 Materials Development

Task-based materials may come from several sources. The best ones are produced by specialists working in the educational context where the materials will be used (Long, 2015). Having invested time and effort in a comprehensive needs analysis, program administrators, curriculum coordinators, and teachers, along with their collaborators, will be ideally positioned to develop suitable in-house materials. Should the time or resources be lacking to develop custom materials, there are several other possibilities. These constitute practical solutions to the challenge of getting started with TBLT:

• Integrate task-based materials found in general teacher training guides into lessons. Many examples of tasks have been published in teaching handbooks or activity books, such as Anderson and McCutcheon's (2019). Containing dozens of example tasks, lesson notes, and ready-to-use materials, this volume is for busy English teachers (for learners at CEFR A2 to C1 level).

• Similar to the previous suggestion, if available, consult domestically published teaching guides. These present tasks that can be used to support the goals of specific national curricula. For examples geared toward the Japanese context, see Kato, Matsumura, and Wickings' (2020) work. For a similar account from Germany, see Müller-Hartmann and Schocker-von Ditfurth's (2011) book.

- Adopt commercially available task-based textbooks. For example, Benevides and Valvona's (2018) textbook contains six units of spoken and written materials, each culminating in an outcome intended for teacher and/or peer assessment. It focuses on business English by presenting product development and marketing scenarios (for learners at or above CEFR B1 level). As another example, *On Task* (Harris & Leeming, 2018) is a textbook series with three levels (High A1 to B1).
- Try out communicative tasks available through the Internet. For instance, at the TBLT Language Learning Task Bank website (Gurzynski-Weiss & IATBLT, n.d.; see also Gurzynski-Weiss, 2021), one can search and download materials created by teachers and researchers.
- Modify existing materials. Willis and Willis (2007) suggested that textbooks often contain tasks without explicitly labeling them as such. Once teachers identify these incognito tasks, they could build on them by adding specific goals, planning time, or a posttask report.
- Make use of sample task-based lesson plans used by teachers, such as those in Willis and Willis's (2007, Appendix 1) work.
- Read about specific applications of TBLT. The chapters in Shehadeh and Coombe (2010) usefully described applications of TBLT in terms of the authors' (1) teaching context, (2) curriculum, tasks, and materials, and (3) reflections.

Any of these approaches might also stimulate discussion among teachers to develop additional materials appropriate for their own local contexts.

The influence of technology on language teaching in general and TBLT in particular cannot be overstated. Many publications have offered examples of how tasks can be implemented through technology (e.g., González-Lloret & Ortega, 2014a; González-Lloret, 2016; Seedhouse, 2017; Thomas & Reinders, 2010). This integration has been described as technology-mediated TBLT (González-Lloret & Ortega, 2014b, pp. 5–9), which requires close consideration of both sides of the TBLT–technology equation in order to: (1) utilize TBLT-informed definitions; (2) be aware of the transformative implications of technology on learning; and (3) articulate relationships between technology, tasks, and curricula. Following from this, González-Lloret (2014, 2016) distinguished between pedagogic language tasks (PLTs) and pedagogic technology tasks (PTTs). The former focus on language whereas the latter comprise the language as well as the technologies and digital literacies employed to accomplish a task. For example, learners can be instructed on appropriate language use in a business letter (a PLT), or this instruction can be integrated into a presentation of relevant email tools and skills (a PTT). Emerging technologies will necessitate continual revision of materials as long as these new tools are required to fulfill learners' needs.

Perusing existing, published task-based materials or lesson plans is often a useful way to understand task-based teaching. In Section 2.4, an account of task-based instruction is described and briefly critiqued.

2.4 Teaching

The use of tasks in classroom practice affords opportunities to redefine teaching and reshape the learning environment. The most influential framework for task-based teaching comes from Willis (1996), who divided instructor roles into three phases that promote increased student involvement and reposition the teacher as a guide. First, in the *pretask phase*, the teacher introduces the topic and, along with the class, explores the content of the task by, for example, brainstorming vocabulary. Here, learners are expected to orient receptively to and activate language that will be useful in performing the task. Models may optionally be provided in the form of teacher demonstrations, audio- or video-recordings of the task being done, or relevant written texts. This phase culminates with the teacher providing instructions about what the students should do in the main phase, including a clear statement of the goal. If applicable, the teacher can announce the amount of time allocated to performance. As an example, in Newton and Bui's (2018) implementation study of TBLT in primary school EFL lessons in Vietnam, pretask work involved (1) brainstorming school subjects to prime relevant vocabulary and (2) listening to a conversation modeling the task while completing a handout.

In the second phase, called the *task cycle*, the students carry out the task as the teacher monitors them. There are three distinct stages to this cycle: task, planning, and report. During the task stage, the teacher must step out of the limelight to allow students to independently perform the task. At this stage, only minimal teacher action is called for, which may include encouraging students who need it, noticing the particular dynamics of student or group performance for later reference, and keeping time. The planning stage follows the task and provides students with time and resources to prepare a report on their task performance. This report may concern the process or outcome of the task. Here, the teacher needs to provide further instructions and advice on language. Finally, during the report stage, the teacher manages the process by selecting groups, taking notes as students share their reports, and then summarizing the key points. In the case of Newton and Bui (2018), during the main phase, students undertook an information gap task to share details about two timetables and then had to identify three differences and two similarities across the timetables. Subsequently, three pairs of students were chosen to publicly perform this main task.

The third and final phase of Willis' framework is the *language focus*, which comprises analysis and practice. This phase is based on a comparison of the students' performance with similar models. As these contain semantic, lexical, or phonological features inherent to the task, they serve as a starting point for raising awareness of language. Students are encouraged to search these models and notice particular linguistic aspects, with the stipulation that "they need to test their own hypotheses and make their own discoveries" (Willis, 1996, p. 103). The teacher now addresses individual questions, which are expected to vary according to students' previous language knowledge. To follow up, oral or written practice of the features students focus on is recommended. This phase was accomplished in Newton and Bui's (2018) setting through teacher-led focus on form and additional language practice in the form of a game.

Willis' tripartite framework has value for helping teachers acclimate to task-based teaching. In particular, the study by Newton and Bui showed the flexibility and viability of such a structure when teachers are transitioning from traditional PPP (presentation, practice, production/performance) to newer TBLT lessons. More recent alternatives build on this model, such as the description in Ellis and colleagues' (2019) work, which consists of pretask options, main-task options, and posttask options. These authors also helpfully noted that the participatory structure of lessons in TBLT varies. Namely, at different points, learners may (1) work individually, (2) collaborate in pairs/groups, or (3) present to the class, and, at times, (4) teachers may lead the lesson. In light of Willis' careful articulation of task-based teaching, further commentary has expanded on the teacher's role (see Norris, 2009; Samuda, 2001, 2015; Van den Branden, 2016; Vandommele, Van den Branden, & Van Gorp, 2018; and Section 5 of this Element).

2.5 Assessment

In task-based language assessment (TBLA), "learners have to use their second language (L2) abilities to get things done" (Norris & East, 2022, p. 507; see also Norris, 2016). This approach is a radical departure from traditional tests that require learners only to demonstrate their second language skills, often rather differently from the ways we ordinarily use language. For instance, a multiple-choice vocabulary test that asks students to read a word, then choose the equivalent item in their first language (L1) is not a task-based test. Alternatively, in TBLA, tests can be designed to measure learners' abilities to use the language they have been learning in class in situations that are potentially relevant to them. For example, in the context of Hong Kong schools, task-based assessments of English ability have been designed which ask students to (1) listen to a recording of the members of a community youth club discussing what to buy for their annual trip to the beach and then (2) complete a shopping list with the items and quantities referred to (Chow & Li, 2008).

Since the mid-1990s, researchers such as Brindley (1994) have commented on the potential of such assessments, noting as key advantages their: (1) underlying conceptualization of language as a tool; (2) integration of assessment with content; (3) use of explicit task criteria to provide diagnostic feedback; and (4) communication of outcomes to stakeholders in terms of performance. The aforementioned 'shopping list' example reflects these characteristics, in that language is used to achieve a real-world goal (i.e., preparing for trip to the beach), there is age-appropriate content, clear criteria can be established according to whether test-takers correctly list each item and quantity, and their degree of success can be communicated based on these criteria. Brindley also noted practical obstacles, including the efforts involved in developing TBLAs and training educators (who may be unaccustomed to such practices) to maximize their benefits. For those seeking to integrate TBLA into classroom instruction, Chow and Li (2008) is a valuable practical resource, especially owing to its numerous activities, which explain the purpose and types of assessment, invite readers to critique sample assessments, and cover practicalities such as scoring, feedback, and using criteria, as well as self and peer-assessment tools.

Two further examples from the literature illustrate how, like other types of assessment, the uses of TBLA can be described as either summative or formative. Formative refers to assessment *for* learning during ongoing instruction, while summative refers to high-stakes assessment *of* learning after instruction.

First, Weaver (2012) described the application of a formative assessment cycle in a task-based business presentation course for university students in Japan. The task was for students to deliver a PowerPoint presentation of a stock listed on the New York Stock Exchange that they thought would be a good investment. Across five class meetings, the instructor led forty-six students to complete a number of steps, including: (1) listening to a description of the assessment cycle; (2) watching a video of a student performing the task; (3) collaboratively discussing the task definition and developing rating criteria (i.e., English speaking skills and presentation design skills); (4) evaluating additional task videos using these criteria; and (5) delivering their own video-recorded presentations, which were rated by their classmates. After this, the teacher (6) analyzed these scores to provide an overall summary of the performances; (7)

met with each student to discuss their scores on the criteria; (8) had the students transcribe their performances; and, finally (9) provided additional feedback on these transcriptions.

Second, as an example of research oriented to *summative* purposes, Youn (2018) employed roleplay tasks to gauge how much pragmatic competence examinees displayed. In this study, 102 English as a second language (ESL) students in the United States carried out five roleplay tasks based on scenarios encountered in academic settings with a trained interlocutor who took the role of a professor or classmate. These audio-recorded performances were then judged using five rating criteria: content delivery, language use, sensitivity to the situation, engaging in interaction, and turn organization (i.e., when and how participants organize conversational turns). The analysis successfully distinguished examinees according to six levels of pragmatic ability. The author recommended that care be taken in designing roleplays so that various, relevant interactional behaviors can be elicited and assessed and also urged that rating criteria explicitly incorporate descriptions of such behavior. For an earlier example of developing and researching TBLA, see Norris and colleagues' (1998) work plus the companion volume by Brown and colleagues (2002).

2.6 Evaluation

Having considered the main elements of a carefully designed TBLT program (i.e., needs analysis, task sequencing, materials, teaching, and assessment), this section describes program evaluation. Despite numerous studies focused solely on its constituent elements, strong TBLT entails a programmatic view whereby all of these elements are taken into consideration when seeking to determine the effectiveness of TBLT (Norris & Davis, 2022). Program evaluation involves systematically gathering data to judge the effectiveness the program as a whole. It uses an array of research methods suited to the purpose of broadly understanding program outcomes. It also differs from individual research studies because its primary aim is to guide decisions about a program. Norris and Davis (2022, pp. 536–537) delineated several ways in which an evaluation can be focused. These highlighted the following unique aspects of task-based programs: the learning sequences, materials, assessments, teacher and student responses, and alignment with the local context.

For example, Markee (1997) reported on the design, implementation, and evaluation of the curricular and teacher innovation (CATI) project, which promoted TBLT as an innovation within a university EFL program in the United States. Taking a participatory and formative approach to the evaluation stage, the author gathered data from action research, teaching journals, and surveys to address the issue of how instructors, who were teaching assistants enrolled in a teacher education program, responded to the innovation by developing new materials, skills, and values. Among the many detailed results Markee provided, teachers contributed to an eventually large bank of tasks and some of them developed new skills relevant to task-based teaching. However, these teachers were not uniformly in agreement regarding the most efficient classroom discourse strategies for promoting student talk during tasks, which suggested that further realignment of pedagogic values might assist in implementing TBLT. Markee also noted that turnover created difficulty in this context because experienced teachers often help to transmit knowledge and skills to new teachers.

The evaluation by Markee represented one approach of many. Other types of evaluation may be viewed as a matter of comparing TBLT to existing, often traditional, approaches such as PPP (see Shintani, 2016, described in Section 3.3). Having offered a general account of each stage in a task-based curriculum in this section, the next section will describe concrete examples of how practitioners developed task-based programs in specific settings.

3 Task-Based Approaches in Context

Tasks, like any educational innovation, must be adapted to the local environment to be effective (Butler, 2011; McDonough, 2015; Newton, 2022). Based on the postulate that diverse, localized implementations resonate with the idea of a task-based curriculum, this section explores a multiplicity of needs and examines how tasks have been used to address these needs. The cases described, which are arranged alphabetically according to the language of instruction, represent diverse geographical locations and educational settings. The learners differ in age, first language, socioeconomic status, L2 proficiency, and other relevant attributes. Around the globe, whether they teach Chinese to undergraduates in Hawai'i, Zapotec to children in Mexico, or other languages to groups elsewhere, educators dedicated to the linguistic, cognitive, social, and professional development of learners in their communities have found merit in TBLT. As a lingua franca, English is also included but no particular language is given priority, so that a range of language- and culture-specific concerns may be brought to light.

3.1 Chinese

As an example of the feasibility of introducing TBLT via the development of instructional modules, Hill and Tschudi (2011) applied a task-based approach in a blended university program on conversational Mandarin Chinese at the

University of Hawai'i at Mānoa. The authors started with a series of needs analyses, which confirmed that students considered asking for directions to be an important real-world task. Having selected this task scenario as a starting point for the innovation, the authors developed a week-long sequence of online and face-to-face activities informed by task-based methodological principles (Doughty & Long, 2003; Long, 2015). Materials for the course were carefully designed to reflect authentic discourse, which was collected by means of interviews and roleplays with Chinese speakers. Discourse features closely pertaining to asking for and providing directions were identified and used to create teaching materials. These features included the macro discourse structure of the target task, as follows:

1. A asks whether B knows the location
2. If B answers "yes," then B asks whether A will walk, drive, or take public transportation
3. A replies
4. B gives appropriate directions
5. A thanks B

In a blended learning format, teaching is construed as independent, online study as well as face-to-face instruction. Appropriately for this context, support for the task-based approach was integrated using a wide array of technological resources. These included online maps and audio files containing model dialogues, as well as gap-filling exercises to introduce task-relevant language items. After working through these materials, the students met face-to-face to perform a map gap (one kind of information gap) task in pairs. They then completed additional cooperative tasks online to practice understanding and giving directions. Regarding assessment, the final exam was based on interactive test tasks with different partners.

Hill and Tschudi (2011) reported an evaluation of this module consisting of formative and summative dimensions. The formative evaluation pinpointed a need for additional technology resources to support an assessment of real-time interactions in online courses. The summative evaluation included research concerning students' uptake of linguistic features and their attitudes toward the course. The uptake analysis targeted topicalization, renomination, repetition, and modal verbs as features of natural discourse. Based on data from two direction-giving pedagogic tasks used in courses for first- and second-year students, the results showed greater use of these target features among second-year students, but also revealed underuse of certain features (topicalization and repetition). Finally, there was some variation across the two tasks used, which interacted with the student year.

On the whole, these results were viewed positively, because they were achieved through completing meaningful tasks and indicated use of naturally occurring discourse features. Students also expressed satisfaction with various elements of the program, including the integration of educational technology, cultural knowledge, authentic discourse, and their own increased awareness of conversational Chinese. In sum, this was an exemplary study of the teacher-led development of a web-based language course informed by student needs. Given the intense effort across its different stages and the varying nature of the expertise required, Hill and Tschudi recommended collaborating with colleagues to undertake such projects.

3.2 Dutch

The duration and scope of task-based teaching in Flanders, in the north of Belgium, makes it one of the best-known examples of a regional implementation of TBLT. Beginning in the 1990s, educators have transformed Flemish schools at the primary, secondary, and adult levels in order to support immigrants, refugees, and their families in their efforts to learn Dutch and integrate into society. This initiative has been fueled by government education policy and the work of the Centre for Language and Education at the Katholieke Universiteit Leuven. The Centre for Language and Education has assisted hundreds of school teams in the region in implementing task-based syllabuses to meet the language needs of a wide variety of students, including speakers of Dutch as an L1 or L2. This process has resulted in a trove of research offering teacher perspectives on tasks in classroom practice (see, e.g., Van den Branden, 2006, 2015, 2016; Van den Branden, Van Gorp, & Verhelst, 2007; Vandommele, Van den Branden, & Van Gorp, 2018). Over the years, that emphasis has expanded from individual in-service teachers' use of tasks in their own lessons to preservice teacher education and school-wide language policies encouraging collaboration (Van den Branden & Van Gorp, 2021).

Van den Branden (2015) provided a vivid snapshot of the theoretical background to this implementation of TBLT, as well as of three theory-to-practice accounts based on classroom research in primary school settings. The first study described how three teachers all modified, in their own ways, a task in which learners were asked to plan and deliver a radio news program for a fictitious, multilingual country. One teacher emphasized creativity and thus prohibited students from referring to real events. Another took the opposite approach, modeling the task using an authentic news broadcast and expecting students to incorporate features of this genre. Whereas both of these teachers disallowed multiple languages, the third one invited students to decide for themselves whether to go along with the original task's encouragement to use their own languages and relied on students to cooperate in groups. In the second study, student–teacher interactions were observed in order to relate them to students' writing development over one year. Writing was scored in several ways, including communicative effectiveness, accuracy, and complexity. Student progress in writing varied both within and across individuals and some of this variation was attributed to the teacher's individualization of instruction. Namely, the teacher encouraged L1 learners to be creative while asking L2 learners to write shorter, more accurate sentences. The third study dealt with the use of tasks to support Dutch learners in a science project on DNA. The study used a pretest-posttest research design with a control group to measure outcomes and also closely examined classroom processes. A key insight here was that two individual students who made large gains varied considerably in their classroom behavior, or the extent to which they engaged with the teacher.

From these studies, Van den Branden (2015) concluded that what matters for learning is not the task design, or workplan, but instead the interaction that emerges between teachers and students in the classroom, as well as students' own unique motivation, goals, and self-regulation.

3.3 English

There have been questions about the applicability of TBLT in contexts where the target language is not widely spoken, and about its appropriateness for beginning, younger learners. In response to these issues, Shintani (2016) reported on a study carried out with six-year-old, novice English learners in Japan, which compared task-based lessons with more traditional presentation-practice-production (PPP) lessons. The context was a small, privately owned school where students whose parents consented to the study received free English lessons twice per week. Three comparison groups engaged in different, age-appropriate lessons catering to the needs of absolute beginners. In the TBLT group, lessons were based around listen-and-do tasks (see the one-way information gap task in Section 1.4.2) and a bingo game. In the PPP group, they involved choral repetition and picture-naming activities. The control group practiced songs and the alphabet. The results of this carefully designed classroom-based study first illustrated how teacher–learner discourse is qualitatively different in TBLT and then showed its quantitative advantages for acquiring vocabulary and grammar.

First, concerning the qualitative findings, this study's use of conversation analysis to inspect classroom discourse revealed several differences between the TBLT and PPP settings. For instance, both involved initiation-response-feedback

(IRF) exchanges, but these were longer in the TBLT lessons. The types of questions varied, with more teacher-initiated display questions in PPP and more student-initiated referential questions in TBLT. Whereas the teacher had control of the floor in PPP, students had more control over turn-taking in TBLT. Finally, as might be expected, turns occurred in chorus in PPP but not in TBLT.

Second, moving on to the quantitative results, the study employed a battery of pretests before the treatments followed by immediate and delayed posttests to compare outcomes across the groups. Regarding vocabulary, there were four tests covering nouns and adjectives introduced in the TBLT and PPP lessons. The nouns were acquired equally well by learners in both groups. However, the TBLT group outperformed the PPP group on adjectives. In accordance with its focus on communication, in the TBLT lessons adjectives were not pretaught but learned incidentally through meaningful exchanges. Concerning grammar, five tests were used to assess incidental learning of two features: the plural –s and copula *be*. In this case, the results were less robust. Neither group improved in their production of these features. Nonetheless, those in the TBLT classes showed improvement in comprehending plural –s. Shintani (2016, p. 136) suggested that this positive result could be explained by the relevance of the plural to completing the task, as illustrated here:

T: please take the mandarins, mandarins to the supermarket.
S1:   mandarin.
T: right. mandarins.
S2:   one?
T: no.
S3:   two?
T: two?
S2:   three?
T: three, yes. okay? ready? three, two, one, go.
Ss: (show the correct card).

Because the listen-and-do task in this example required the children to listen carefully for the exact number of items, it may have led them to notice plural marking. As a reminder, noticing (Schmidt, 1990) occurs when learners consciously attend to lexical, phonological, grammatical, or other features of L2 input. The nature of the tests used in this study may explain the results for production. In conclusion, Shintani (2016) argued that TBLT is a flexible, communicative option that can be localized to enhance the value of English classes for not only younger but also mature learners in Japan.

3.4 German

A commendable case of grounding curricular thinking in notions of task and genre can be found in Byrnes' work within the Georgetown University German Department (see Byrnes, 2014, 2015; Byrnes, Maxim, & Norris, 2010; Byrnes et al., 2006). Systemic functional linguistics provided the basis for this unique curriculum. This theory views language as a semiotic resource that enacts and construes social contexts by presenting choices that enable users to express (1) what they experience, (2) who is taking part (and their social relations), and (3) the role of language itself. Such expression comprises frequently occurring genres, which are recognizable to communities of language users. Based on the academic and professional needs of its students, the department's curriculum aims to promote longitudinal development to advanced levels through a focus on oral and written genres. This is achieved through genre-oriented, task-based teaching, the gist of which is described by Byrnes (2014, p. 243) as follows:

> In order to perform certain genres, learners need to have access to certain language resources and, in reverse, in order to develop certain language resources, learners must be given the opportunity to perform certain generic tasks that tend to deploy those resources

In a way, Byrnes' (2014) suggestion circumvents the bottleneck problem (see Section 2.1); genres are defined by fixed and flexible language choices, so orienting to them from the outset narrows the scope of a task's linguistic requirements.

In practice, this curriculum spans five levels, which correspond to several years of instruction, depending on whether students are enrolled intensively or nonintensively. Byrnes and colleagues (2006) illustrated how the first four levels were designed to facilitate literacy development along a continuum from personal to public discourses. For instance, among the writing tasks found in Levels I through IV are a personal letter, application letter, *Aufruf* (political appeal), and journalistic report, respectively. Materials used to support learning included vocabulary sheets and functional phrase charts. Detailed assessment guidelines are also provided to students, which spell out criteria related to task, content, and language.

Byrnes' research has explored learners' writing development within this curricular framework. One study utilized longitudinal data from a range of standard and innovative measures to chart student progress in written German (Byrnes, 2014). Concerning Levels I through IV, clear gains in syntactic complexity across the curriculum were found on two of three general measures.

Concerning Levels II through IV, on a measure of lexical density (the ratio of content to function words), very clear increases differentiated each level, which suggested that writers expanded not only the length of their sentences, but also that of their clauses. Further analyses showed large increases in nominalization, realized through the use of grammatical metaphor, especially between Levels III and IV. The author cautiously does not attribute these results solely to the curriculum, instruction, or tasks, but cites in addition the shared philosophy and coordination among program educators, which cannot be taken for granted.

3.5 Spanish

The context for González-Lloret and Nielson (2015) was the US Border Patrol Academy, which provides language training tailored to the needs of agents who must speak fluent Spanish in order to offer assistance, communicate legal rights, and safely resolve conflicts. The TBLT program resulted from dissatisfaction with a previous grammar-based course that left agents-in-training underprepared for these responsibilities. This is a highly informative case as it illustrates how linking all six, interconnected curricular components to the notion of task can improve training programs. First, a needs analysis identified seven target tasks, or job duties likely requiring the L2. Second, these tasks were sequenced to form an eight-week series of increasingly complex modules. Third, materials were developed, including audio- and video-recordings, roleplay scenarios, and an interactive video game. Fourth, regarding teaching, native speakers participated in roleplaying and unscripted practice activities, and instructors were encouraged to use focus on form. Fifth, task-based assessment was used. At the end of each module, instructors evaluated students on task performances they carried out with native speakers, using rubrics that stipulated linguistic competencies linked to specific success criteria (e.g., "using appropriate Spanish, the trainee extracts subject from hiding place", p. 530). The final examination was also performance-based. Several years into the implementation of this program, the sixth component, evaluation, was carried out.

González-Lloret and Nielson (2015) reported three evaluation studies, each of which shed light on key indicators of the effectiveness of the program. Study 1 compared students from the TBLT course with those who had taken the grammar-based course at the academy. Based on an oral picture narration task, measures of fluency, lexical complexity, syntactic complexity, and grammatical accuracy were used. The oral production of those in the TBLT group was significantly more fluent than those in the grammar-based group, and also not less complex or accurate. Study 2 looked at gains in proficiency in the TBLT program only. Students took a computerized oral test at the beginning and end of the course. Over the duration of the program, their scores significantly increased on overall spoken proficiency, as well as on sentence mastery, vocabulary, fluency, and pronunciation. Further analyses demonstrated that the increase in their ability was unrelated to starting proficiency. Study 3 gauged opinions of the program using a questionnaire methodology. Respondents included those who were enrolled in the task-based course, as well as agents who had graduated from it. All of these individuals generally found the program useful, interesting, and relevant. Particularly worth noting is that graduates agreed that they could use the Spanish they learned in the field.

3.6 Zapotec

South of the Mexico–US border, in a very different context, Riestenberg and colleagues (Riestenberg & Sherris, 2018; Riestenberg & Manzano, 2019) have applied task-based principles in teaching Macuiltianguis Zapotec to children living in the community in Oaxaca where this language is traditionally spoken. Because there are fewer younger than older speakers, needs include the preservation of the culture and revitalization of the language. Therefore, the project highlighted the transmission of traditional knowledge and creation of new domains of language use through tasks. Riestenberg and Sherris (2018) elaborated on the role of investment (encompassing identity and ideology) and task-based methodological principles (Long, 2015) in Indigenous language education. Pedagogic tasks in the Zapotec classroom concerned greetings, small talk, and shopping for food. During instruction, teachers used elaborated spoken input (i.e., repetition and paraphrasing) and provided limited, contextually appropriate negative feedback (i.e., recasts) on mispronunciation. These discourse moves facilitate comprehension and production in a new language. Learners also practiced performing tasks in collaboration with native speakers in the community, which fostered their identities as language users and led to further use of Zapotec in new authentic settings, such as sporting events. Assessment was conducted in a culturally appropriate way by adopting a formative approach that fostered "the perception of linguistic knowledge as symbolic capital" (Riestenberg & Sherris, 2018, p. 451). In practice, this involved giving students points for task completion, which could then be exchanged for a prize. In these ways, the program achieved its aim of increasing spoken interaction, although the authors cautiously noted that a long-term commitment is necessary to reach the more ambitious goal of establishing a new generation of speakers.

One way that new spaces for the use of Macuiltianguis Zapotec, a mainly oral language, might be created is through writing. Riestenberg and Manzano (2019) examined how tasks support the development of literacy within this setting, viewing writing as a set of processes embedded within sociocultural contexts, according to Ivanič's model (cited in Riestenberg & Manzano, 2019). This effort built upon those of a revitalization group that has standardized the alphabet and created print resources: a word list, various games, and booklets containing songs, stories, and local history. The following examples illustrate how writing was used as a scaffold for speaking tasks. First, to prepare students for the task of asking a speaker how to prepare a traditional drink, the teacher asked them to listen to the ingredients, write them down, and compare their spelling with a classmate's. The teacher then gave them the spelling and had them label the ingredients on a whiteboard. Second, to prepare the students to introduce themselves at a community event, they first memorized and then were provided with a written sample of a self-introduction, from which they borrowed chunks of language to write their own personalized introduction. In a final example, the students made use of Spanish and Zapotec on signs that they created with slogans promoting Earth Day, which were posted on a nearby highway. As such, in addition to developing phonological and orthographic knowledge, new arenas for the everyday use of Zapotec emerged from the integration of written language and task-based teaching.

Holistic accounts of instruction (such as those above) are invaluable for understanding how various features of educational practice come together when tasks are viewed as primary. To offer another, complementary perspective, Section 4 will introduce several discrete approaches to pedagogic research on tasks.

4 Research into TBLT

This section reviews twenty-five studies of TBLT published in the most recent decade (between 2011 and 2021). First, some good news. Studies comparing TBLT programs to traditional, non-TBLT programs indicate that using tasks leads to stronger gains on L2 outcomes, as well as positive attitudes toward TBLT programs by teachers and learners (Bryfonski & McKay, 2017). Accordingly, this section will focus on studies illustrating the use of tasks in practice, rather than methods comparison studies (see Section 3.3 for instance; for a recent example, see Borro, 2022).

The review is organized into several branches, based on the notion that tasks can be viewed as either static workplans constructed by materials designers or as a series of processes implemented by teachers and learners (e.g., Breen, 1987; Samuda, 2015; Van den Branden, 2016). The main features of the task workplan are design and mode. The primary task processes are preparation, interaction, and repetition. These branches (Figure 4) are each explained, reviewed, and

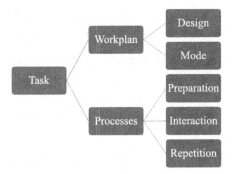

Figure 4 Research foci based on task-as-workplan versus task-in-process

summarized to provide breadth as well as depth. Studies were purposely selected with a view toward providing a balanced treatment of each area (due to space constraints, the review was limited to five representative studies per area). The outcomes that researchers investigated in these studies varied from measures of conversational interaction to individual performance (see Sections 4.1 to 4.6 for details). Measurement of individual learner performance has often involved looking at its complexity, accuracy, and fluency in order to capture dimensions of speech or writing that are relevant to L2 development (for a detailed synthesis, see Skehan & Foster, 2012).

As an initial point of departure, readers may wish to consider: Is the language learning potential of tasks primarily a matter of the stable, abstract properties of the workplan or of the varied, particular processes in which teachers and learners engage?

4.1 Design

As already indicated in Section 1.4, much attention has been paid to the inherent features of tasks as workplans. Present research in this area is an outgrowth of decades of work, beginning in the 1980s, which described and classified tasks according to their essential characteristics (e.g., Nunan, 1989; Prabhu, 1987; Yule, 1997). In the 1990s, researchers began to consolidate various pedagogic task types into systematic frameworks (Pica, Kanagy, & Falodun, 1993; Skehan, 1996) which referenced key considerations in SLA, such as the essential roles of negotiated interaction and psycholinguistic processing. The turn of the millennium brought with it research seeking to refine and test theoretical models of the influence of task design on L2 performance and learning, especially Skehan's Limited Attentional Capacity Model and Robinson's Cognition Hypothesis (for state-of-the-art commentaries, see Skehan, 2018 and Robinson, 2015).

The latter approach, focused on here due to space limitations, is based on Robinson's Triadic Componential Framework, which differentiates between:

1. task complexity, or cognitive factors[2] that direct or disperse language processing resources
2. task conditions, or interactive factors concerning participation or participants
3. task difficulty, or learner factors related to ability or affect.

As a teacher-friendly example, Michel (2011) designed tasks presenting adult L2 learners of Dutch with a scenario wherein they had to decide which of the contestants on a dating show would make the best couple, based on their age, hobbies, and other characteristics. There was a simple version with four contestants and a complex version with six contestants. In this example, increasing the number of contestants is assumed to increase cognitive task complexity, with beneficial consequences for L2 output, interaction, and learning.

Studies on task complexity using this framework have typically looked at whether various features of task design make a difference in terms of learners' language use during spoken or written performance. In the case of speaking, the effects may differ, and have been investigated separately, for monologic (i.e., narrative) or dialogic (i.e., interactive) performance. There are meta-analytic reviews describing the effects on spoken monologic (Jackson & Suethanapornkul, 2013) and written (Johnson, 2017) language production. These studies have helped to identify which task design variables have been most widely investigated. For instance, across studies of their effects on spoken and written performance, research had mainly looked at the influence of the following resource-directing features of task complexity: number of elements, reasoning demands, and whether the task was to be performed in here-and-now or there-and-then conditions. Importantly, these studies also bring to light small, yet meaningful effects of task complexity on L2 production across the literature. For instance, increasing task complexity influences oral narrative production by raising accuracy ($d = 0.28$; CI = ± 0.12) and lowering fluency ($d = -0.16$; CI = ± 0.09) (Jackson & Suethanapornkul, 2013).[3] The focus here on interactive tasks is intentional, as this line of research has received less attention despite its relevance to instruction.

The findings from several studies into the effects of task design on learner–learner interaction in pairs or groups (see Table 2) are briefly summarized here. To begin with face-to-face studies, Révész (2011) showed that learners

---

[2] These factors include resource-directing variables, which make conceptual/cognitive demands, as well as contrasting resource-dispersing variables (e.g., planning time) which make performative/procedural demands (Robinson, 2022, p. 211).

[3] Cohen's *d* is a measure of effect size that indicates how large or small a difference was found between groups or across time.

Table 2 Studies on simple versus complex interactive task design

Study	Location	Setting	Learners	Task(s)
Révész (2011)	United States	University	L1 various/L2 English	To allocate funds to community programs in NYC
Kim (2012)	South Korea	University	L1 Korean/L2 English	To roleplay finding part-time work, being a matchmaker, discussing a promotion, hiring employees
Kim & Taguchi (2015)	South Korea	Junior high school	L1 Korean/L2 English	To complete a drama script by adding a dialogue to a picture
Solon, Long, & Gurzynski-Weiss (2017)	United States	University	L1 English/ L2 Spanish	To complete a tour map with missing information
Adams, Alwi, & Newton (2015)	Malaysia	University	L1 various/L2 English	To compare and recommend engineering software

produced more lexically diverse (but less syntactically complex) language in complex versus simple tasks. She also found more language-related episodes (LREs), in which learners spontaneously discuss language they are using, in complex tasks. Focusing on question formation, Kim (2012) also investigated LREs. Learners doing ++complex tasks produced the greatest number of LREs, whereas +complex tasks generated more LREs than simple tasks. Furthermore, the percentage of students showing question development increased according to the task design from 67 percent in the simple group to 72 percent in the +complex group to 82 percent in the ++complex group. In Kim and Taguchi's (2015) study, learners in the complex group produced more LREs about certain pragmatic features than those in the simple group. Both these treatment groups outperformed a control group on a written discourse completion test of pragmatic knowledge on immediate posttests. The complex group also did better than either of the other groups on a delayed posttest. Solon, Long, and Gurzynski-Weiss (2017) found that learner production of pronunciation-focused LREs was not different across simple versus complex tasks. However, production of the Spanish /e/ vowel sound was more nativelike when performing a complex task. As an extension of the research in face-to-face settings, turning to computer-mediated communication (CMC), Adams, Alwi, and Newton (2015) reported that a simple task, which provided further instructions on the procedure and a comparison table, led to more accurate written production than a complex task that withheld this support.

In the aforementioned studies, complex task versions were carefully created by adding reasoning demands, increasing the number of elements, or removing structural support. It appears that such modifications to task design can, in ways more or less in keeping with Robinson's Cognition Hypothesis, impact immediate learning opportunities and longitudinal language development. To summarize:

- In theory, during complex interactive tasks, learner L2 production should display greater accuracy and more interaction, in the form of confirmation checks and clarification requests (Robinson, 2015).
- Complex tasks have been found to yield less accurate grammar but also more accurate pronunciation, so their effect on accuracy remains unclear.
- More complex tasks generate more LREs. This suggests that complex tasks facilitate interaction among learners to address language issues. It might also imply a greater need for teacher intervention, should learners need expert assistance to resolve LREs.

- Over time, the challenges posed by complex tasks may be more suited than simple tasks and traditional instruction to the development of syntactic and pragmatic features.

Instructors ought to take note of such differences and plan sequences of engaging and appropriately challenging tasks.

4.2 Mode

Mode refers to whether communication is oral or written, and includes hybrid modes having characteristics of both speech and writing, such as CMC. In practice, tasks may be conducted entirely in a single mode (e.g., oral discussions versus written essays) or they may involve more than one mode (e.g., note-taking based on a lecture). This might be considered a part of the task's design, but it is also independent of it, because a given task can sometimes be carried out in different modes. For example, L2 learners in a business program might practice offering a position to a successful job candidate via either a spoken message left on an answering machine or a written email, with a given number of details required to be conveyed regardless of the mode. Problematically, the language teaching field has strongly tended to associate tasks with oral communication, as shown by much of the literature dating back to the 1990s and earlier. According to Byrnes and Manchón (2014), this dominant emphasis on the oral mode continues to permeate task-based theory, research, and practice. It is therefore highly appropriate that recent research has shifted to look at the contribution of the written mode to learning in tasks, as well as to how task-based studies might inform our understanding of L2 writing. In connection with this shift, studies have begun to investigate task modality effects (e.g., Kormos, 2014; Kuiken & Vedder, 2011; Tavakoli, 2014).

In their commentary on mode, Gilabert, Manchón, and Vasylets (2016) define and situate mode within a model of orality-literacy, discuss relationships between mode and stages in L2 learning, and conclude by calling for further research on mode as an option in task design and, in particular, research on the effect of modality on input processing in tasks. They share a key assumption, found throughout the literature, that different modes offer different learning potential. This idea is based on close consideration of the inherent qualities of speaking versus writing. Speech is heard, rapidly delivered, ephemeral, typically involves two or more interlocutors, combines with nonverbal information such as gestures to convey meaning, and provides opportunities for immediate feedback. In contrast, writing is seen, slower paced, permanent, addressed to distant audiences, and offers more opportunities to draw upon explicit

Table 3 Studies on oral versus written modes

Study	Location	Setting	Learners	Task(s)
Kuiken & Vedder (2011)	Netherlands	University	L1 Dutch/L2 Italian	To recommend a holiday destination to a friend
Kormos (2014)	Hungary	Secondary school	Hungarian–English bilinguals/English learners	To narrate a comic strip; to create a story based on pictures
Tavakoli (2014)	United Kingdom	Private language school	L1 various/L2 English	To narrate a story based on pictures
Vasylets, Gilabert, & Manchón (2017)	Spain	University	Spanish–Catalan bilinguals/L2 English	To explain life-saving actions during a crisis based on pictures of a building on fire
Ziegler & Phung (2019)	Vietnam	University	L1 Vietnamese/L2 English	To describe pictures to a partner based on a story

knowledge and external resources, such as dictionaries. Another important point raised by Gilabert, Manchón, and Vasylets is that, though it may at times be helpful to consider the contributions of speaking and writing separately, pedagogic tasks often engage learners in a blending of modes, including speaking-to-write and writing-to-speak. The real-world tasks learners aspire to may frequently blend oral and written communication. Therefore, TBLT researchers and practitioners should attend to the dynamic permutation of modes found within and across tasks for the sake of authenticity.

A few relevant studies (see Table 3) are summarized here. In the first four studies in this table, researchers compared narrative tasks carried out in spoken and written modalities in terms of the complexity and accuracy of L2 production. The final study in the table investigated how an interactive task under different modes of CMC yielded distinct opportunities for learning. The analyses in Kuiken and Vedder (2011) mainly addressed task complexity effects, which were similar across modes, but their descriptive results indicated greater syntactic complexity and lexical diversity in the written mode, as well as fewer errors in the oral mode. Kormos (2014) directly compared spoken and written performances, finding that the latter were stronger in terms of lexical variety, lexical complexity, accuracy, and use of noun phrase modifiers. In contrast, spoken performances were stronger on measures of cohesion. Tavakoli's (2014) study used simple and complex tasks. The results indicated that, in the simpler task design, learners produced more syntactically complex structures in writing versus speaking, though the more complex task showed no such differences across modes. In a large-scale study, Vasylets, Gilabert, and Manchón (2017) found main effects for both task complexity and mode. The written task performances were higher in lexical, structural, and propositional complexity, whereas no mode-related difference was found in accuracy. Lastly, considering the influence of mode during interaction in CMC, Ziegler and Phung (2019) compared four modes available via Skype: text, audio, video, and multimodal. Tasks performed using multimodal chat showed the greatest percentage of all interactional features, including negotiation, recasts, and explicit feedback. The video mode had the second highest percentage for nearly all features.

Mode is a relevant consideration in language classrooms. To recap, the findings suggest the following:

- Mode influences L2 narrative production and interaction during task performance.
- These effects appear to be independent of task design, although the possibility remains that the effect of mode and complexity are interrelated.

- In narrative tasks, the written mode tends to show more syntactic and lexical complexity than the oral mode.
- Learners may be aware of differences in these modes and use their L2 differently in speaking versus writing tasks.
- In interactive CMC tasks, oral modes supported by video technology are more suited to the negotiation of meaning as they afford access to nonverbal signals.

These results should encourage teachers to think carefully about mode when planning task-based instruction. In addition, they suggest that learners should have opportunities to demonstrate their L2 abilities in different modes, at different times. However, there are certain limitations to note, as well. First, it should be kept in mind that challenges arise when seeking to compare performance across the distinctive modes of speaking and writing, particularly with regard to the amount of time taken. Second, it is of utmost importance in TBLT to remain faithful to the mode in which the task is most likely to be performed in the real world, including tasks which blend modes (Gilabert, Manchón, & Vasylets, 2016). In light of these issues, teachers might find it easier to adjust the degree of task complexity than to render a task typically done in speaking as a writing task, or vice versa. Despite these caveats, the studies reviewed here generally reflect bottom-up concerns because the teaching of writing and literacy skills is a major area of language instruction. Fortunately, the lack of attention to this area in TBLT has begun to be addressed (Byrnes & Manchón, 2014). Moreover, these studies were generally clear about task design, content, and procedures and forthcoming as regards pedagogic implications. Put succinctly, as Vasylets, Gilabert, and Manchón (2017) concluded, "mode may mediate the way in which L2 learners use their linguistic knowledge" (p. 422).

4.3 Preparation

The discussion of task processes, or those factors that play out directly in the classroom, begins with the question of how teachers and learners can prepare together before a task. Section 2.4 has already introduced the framework offered by Willis (1996), noting that the pretask phase may involve discussing the task's topic and content, brainstorming useful language, analyzing models of successful task performance, and establishing expectations for the main task phase, among other forms of preparation. A related, useful concept from recent research is that of task readiness.

As proposed by Bui (2014), readiness for a task consists of implicit and explicit types of planning. Implicit planning includes a learner's inherent familiarity with content (e.g., professional knowledge), schema (e.g., routines used during the task), and the task itself. Learners may gain certain advantages when their knowledge of these areas is activated. Teachers should therefore try to leverage student familiarity with task content and schema, as Willis (1996) recommended. Otherwise, the benefit of this type of readiness may not extend to task performance. This view is also consistent with the use of motivational strategies as preparation. During the preactional stage of task motivation (Dörnyei, 2002), for instance, the teacher helps to orient students to goals, convey intentions behind the task, and initiate purposeful action.

Another kind of readiness according to Bui (2014) is explicit planning, which involves externally imposed forms of planning. The options here include pretask planning and within-task planning. Based on Ellis (2005), pretask planning, or planning that ensues prior to task performance, includes rehearsal and strategic planning. The former involves practicing a task. The latter encourages students to carefully think about what they want to say and how they will say it. Pretask planning differs from within-task planning, which concerns the amount of time allocated to the task. Providing more or less time for performance naturally influences the amount of planning time available to learners within a task. As shown in Section 4.2, there are differences across the oral and written mode in this respect. In practice, these two broad types of explicit planning can be combined to yield lessons using distinct combinations of planning conditions (e.g., +/- pretask planning and +/- within-task planning).

A further distinction for instructors to be aware of is whether strategic pretask planning is guided or unguided. For instance, Mochizuki and Ortega (2008) described a study carried out with groups of EFL learners at a high school in Japan who were asked to retell a picture story. The unguided and guided planning groups were given the same amount of time to prepare; however, the guided planning group was also given a handout on relative clause formation and told that it might be useful for the task, but they could only use it during planning. The results showed large effects in favor of the guided planners on both the quantity and quality of relative clauses produced, with no significant difference in fluency between groups. This study shows that the processes undertaken during planning are essential. From the perspective of the classroom, an obvious question is how learners may support each other during the process of preparing for a task. Finally, another approach to preparation involves metacognitive instruction to enhance students' learning opportunities during interactive tasks (Fujii, Ziegler, & Mackey, 2016).

Table 4 summarizes details from a handful of studies on learners preparing for tasks. The first two studies looked into individual planning. Bui (2014) gave students no planning time versus ten-minutes planning time before speaking about familiar versus unfamiliar topics. Planning time improved complexity

Table 4 Studies on preparation and planning for tasks

Study	Location	Setting	Learners	Task(s)
Bui (2014)	Hong Kong	University	L1 Cantonese/L2 English	To describe the process of virus transmission
Van de Guchte et al. (2019)	Netherlands	Secondary school	L1 Dutch/L2 German	To describe a school cafeteria
Kang & Lee (2019)	South Korea	Secondary school	L1 Korean/L2 English	To write a story based on pictures
Lee & Burch (2017)	United States	University	L1 various/L2 English	To give a presentation based on research
Sato (2020)	Chile	Secondary school	L1 Spanish/L2 English	To exchange personal opinions on controversial issues

and familiarity enhanced accuracy. Both kinds of readiness promoted fluency. Next, Van de Guchte and colleagues (2019) prepared students by first having them watch videos of peer-models carrying out a task while focusing on either a specific language feature, or the persuasiveness of the content. These groups were given two posttests during which they performed a narrative. The language group was more accurate (only on posttest 1), whereas the content group produced more complex structures (on both posttests). The next two studies expand the focus to collaborative planning. Kang and Lee (2019) studied the effects of individual versus collaborative (i.e., paired) planning conditions. Students first did a writing task after a set amount of unguided, individual planning time and then performed an equivalent task after planning with a self-selected partner. Fluency and complexity improved after collaborative planning, during which learners mainly discussed useful words and expressions. Accuracy was unaffected by planning condition. In contrast to studies measuring the complexity, accuracy, and fluency of L2 production, Lee and Burch (2017) showed that collaborative planning involves learner-relevant social processes. Three students engaged in negotiation of their own group's plan through various proposals, agreements, and disagreements, while discussing a handout presenting them with a workplan for a week-long research project. Beyond orienting them to form or content, this required them to attend to their roles and responsibilities as group members progressing toward the shared goal of task completion. Lastly, Sato (2020) investigated how metacognitive instruction for collaborative interaction (MICI) can prepare learners to reap the benefits of tasks. Learners in the MICI group, who participated in a multistage intervention targeting collaborative strategies, used more appeals, clarification requests, and comprehension checks during task interaction and outperformed both controls and a task-only group on a posttest measure of comprehensibility.

Preparation is a crucial stage, which must not be overlooked. The following are some key findings from this section:

- Before monologic speaking tasks, when compared to no time, ten minutes of pretask planning time improves fluency and complexity. Other options such as guided planning and familiarity may improve accuracy.
- Before dialogic speaking tasks, targeted metacognitive instruction can promote learner engagement and enhance comprehensibility during spontaneous production.
- Before group presentations, providing detailed workplans helps learners to orient to their roles, which can facilitate work being carried out smoothly.
- Before writing tasks, having learners pair up to actively discuss their ideas can improve their fluency and complexity, if not their accuracy.

Given the wide range of options, these findings are tentative conclusions which, ideally, will be augmented by future research. Metacognitive instruction (Sato, 2020; see also Fujii, Ziegler, & Mackey, 2016) appears to be one of the most promising avenues, particularly in foreign language settings. Planning studies highlight learner involvement in TBLT, given the clear effects it has on improving language performance, comprehensibility, and interaction.

4.4 Interaction

Conversational interaction assists the development of L2 knowledge because it fosters comprehension, provides feedback, and encourages output (see, e.g., Behney & Gass, 2021; Long, 1996; Mackey, 2007, 2012, 2020; Philp, Adams, & Iwashita, 2013; Pica, 1994). In L2 classroom settings, particularly during pair and group work, interaction research has focused on the negotiation of meaning, which occurs during conversations where a listener works to repair understanding of a speaker's intended meaning by using clarification requests (*what do you mean?*) or confirmation checks (*you said ten-fifteen not ten-fifty, right?*), or when a speaker attempts to find out whether an utterance is understood by the listener using a comprehension check (*do you understand?*). These speaker/listener roles may be adopted by teachers or learners. Interaction research has also examined the negotiation of form through corrective feedback provided to learners by teachers using recasts, elicitations, or metalinguistic explanations to follow up on erroneous L2 production. Tasks create opportunities for these forms of interaction and studies viewing interaction as a catalyst for L2 acquisition have often relied on tasks.

For instance, important work by Keck and colleagues (2006) summarized the results of fourteen studies that had investigated the impact that communication tasks have on the acquisition of specific grammatical or lexical features by adult L2 learners. The tasks used in these studies included the five types described by Pica, Kanagy, and Falodun (1993; see Section 1.4 of this Element), as well as narrative/story-telling tasks incorporating interaction. In these quantitative studies, the impact of task-based interaction was assessed using test scores. Keck and colleagues' meta-analytic study used standardized measures of these scores to combine results from the entire set of primary studies. There were clear outcomes in favor of task-based interaction. In terms of its immediate effectiveness, the average effect when comparing task-based versus control groups was large ($d = 0.92$; CI = ± 0.24). Considering the duration of these effects, results varied according to the delay between the treatment and the test. A short delay (eight to twenty-nine days later) yielded a large average effect within a narrow range ($d = 1.12$; CI = ± 0.31). A longer delay (thirty to sixty days later) yielded a similar, large average effect, within a wider range ($d = 1.18$; CI = ± 0.83). That is, the observed positive effects remained large but became less precise as time went on. This pattern could be due to the fact that fewer studies investigated the long-term effects of task-based interaction on SLA. Nonetheless, the findings clearly demonstrate the contribution of task-based interaction to grammar and lexis.

Given the effectiveness of interaction, new research directions have emerged. In terms of explanatory variables, the interactionist agenda has looked to the unique contributions of learners, instructors, and other interlocutors (Gurzynski-Weiss, 2017) for insight, including studies on cognitive individual differences (see Mackey, 2020 for a review). Another recent development, exemplified by studies using conversation analysis (e.g., Kunitz & Skogmyr Marian, 2017; Ro, 2018) or those grounded in engagement (e.g., Baralt, Gurzynski-Weiss, & Kim, 2016; Philp & Duchesne, 2016), is increased attention to the interplay between task-based interaction and social or psychological processes. In light of these trends, the studies reviewed in Table 5 focused on what learners bring to their interactions and how they experience them.

Factors such as age and proficiency make a difference in how students interact, as do their roles. Among groups of younger (five-to-seven-year-old) and older (eleven-to-twelve-year-old) children, Oliver, Philp, and Duchesne (2017) found that primary students supported each other to complete a set of information gap tasks. Several age-related differences emerged, with more language play among the younger group and more cooperation and on-task behavior among the older group, though task effects were also found to influence these outcomes. Turning to proficiency, Dao and McDonough (2017) had adult learners do a task in mixed-level pairs. They gave either the lower- or higher-proficiency student the role of information holder versus information receiver. When the less proficient partner had to convey the information, pairs engaged in more LREs, though no difference occurred in how these were resolved. These pairs also demonstrated higher mutuality, which refers to collaborative or expert/novice dynamics thought to be beneficial for L2 learning (see Storch, 2002). Roles were also the focus of Le's (2021) study, in which university students joined an academic reading circle in a different role each week: leader, notetaker, luminary (responsible for teaching words from the text), or contextualizer (responsible for making connections based on the text). Analyses showed how students used their roles to orient to performance and problematize interactions. Suggestions for minimizing the challenges of certain roles included simplifying or modeling the task, as well as checking to ensure progress.

Table 5 Studies on interacting during tasks

Study	Location	Setting	Learners	Task(s)
Oliver, Philp, & Duchesne (2017)	Australia	Primary school	L1 various/L2 English	To talk about animals, shapes, and sports
Dao & McDonough (2017)	Vietnam	University	L1 Vietnamese/L2 English	To watch a video, retell the story, and cowrite it with an original ending
Le (2021)	United States	University	L1 various/L2 English	To discuss an academic text in groups
Aubrey (2017)	Japan	University	L1 Japanese/L2 English	To exchange information and make a decision
Nakamura, Phung, & Reinders (2021)	Thailand	University	L1 mostly Thai/L2 English	To discuss and choose three buildings to add to campus

Turning to sociopsychological outcomes, learner experiences of flow or engagement appear to depend on the interactional context. Aubrey (2017) studied flow experiences (e.g., challenge-skill balance, concentration, and enjoyment) among Japanese learners in intracultural versus intercultural pairings. The latter group, who interacted with non-Japanese international students, consistently reported more flow-enhancing experiences and fewer flow-inhibiting ones across a series of five communicative tasks. Lastly, Nakamura, Phung, and Reinders (2021) investigated how choice influences interaction by creating two versions of a task: one that gave learners predetermined options to discuss and another that let them choose their own options to discuss with their group. The version allowing for more choice led to greater engagement, as measured using cognitive, behavioral, social, and emotional indices (see also Lambert, Philp, & Nakamura, 2017).

In sum, learners influence task-based interaction in at least these ways:

- Age and maturity influence children's social worlds and their interactions. Tasks should be designed specifically for children in order to sustain their interest. Younger learners engage in play and conflict more than older peers.
- Proficiency will naturally influence the amount of L2 input, feedback, and output generated. Mixed proficiency dyads can be effective when the lower proficiency partner is required to share information and the higher proficiency partner must request it.
- Roles create expectations about the task which can guide performance and lead to group management. Teachers can assist by assigning or helping learners choose roles, modeling them, and checking that they are carried out efficiently.

Also, in addition to fostering their L2 development, interacting in tasks influences learners:

- Matching learners with those from different cultural backgrounds may increase their experience of flow, thereby creating optimal classroom experiences.
- Giving learners choices may enhance their engagement, which encompasses cognitive, behavioral, affective, and social dimensions of learning.

4.5 Repetition

Unlike the areas reviewed up to this point, task repetition is a relatively recent area of empirical interest. Bygate (2018) presented the first edited collection covering the topic. In the editor's introductory chapter, it is pointed out that a task can never be precisely repeated. There will always be at least some slight variation in a learner's performance owing to the fluctuating psychological and social conditions under which it is carried out. For this reason, Larsen-Freeman (2018) proposed replacing the term *repetition* with *iteration*, in order to better convey that the rationale for doing tasks again is, indeed, to promote change and L2 development, rather than to have learners reproduce their speech or writing verbatim.

Bygate (2018) also helpfully summarized early research on task repetition, drawing three conclusions from a spate of studies that began in the early 1990s. Specifically, all studies had found some significant differences based on repeating tasks. It was found that these effects occurred regardless of age or proficiency. And it was not possible to predict which of three dimensions of L2 production (complexity, accuracy, or fluency) would mainly be affected by repetition. There is thus an ongoing need for research into this key area of TBLT, which can have practical implications. To illustrate how much ground there is to cover, Bygate also identified various types of partial repetition occurring in educational contexts: tasks can hold some feature (such as the design or material) constant, but vary in terms of the interlocutor, the arrangement of the material, the number of contents, the response, or the mode, and so forth. For example, a map gap task can be redone with students navigating different routes or locations, addressing different partners, using maps of the same location at a different scale, adding obstacles to the path, or reducing the time allowed, and so on. The studies summarized in Table 6 were recent attempts to address the panoply of ways that tasks can be repeated.

The first two studies in Table 6 used monologic tasks. Ahmadian and Tavakoli (2011) compared four conditions based on planning type (careful vs. pressured) and repetition (with vs. without). In the repetition conditions, the task was repeated after one week. It was found that careful planning in combination with repetition led to improved performance on measures of complexity, accuracy, and fluency. Thai and Boers (2016) compared learners who repeated monologues in a constant time group (2/2/2 minutes) with a shrinking time group (3/2/1 minutes). Despite the popularity of 3/2/1-type activities among practitioners, this study revealed that although the shrinking time condition benefitted fluency, it also seemed to inhibit planning to enhance complexity and accuracy, which was evident under the constant time condition. The remaining three studies used interactive tasks. Kim and Tracy-Ventura (2013) looked at the differences between exact repetition (same procedure, same content) and procedural repetition (same procedure, new content). Based on three iterations spanning one week, they reported few significant differences between these groups on measures of complexity, fluency, and accuracy. Procedural repeaters

Table 6 Studies on repeating tasks

Study	Location	Setting	Learners	Task(s)
Ahmadian & Tavakoli (2011)	Iran	English language center	L1 Persian/L2 English	To watch a short film and give a narration of the story
Thai & Boers (2016)	Vietnam	High school	L1 Vietnamese/L2 English	To talk about one's favorite movie
Kim & Tracy-Ventura (2013)	South Korea	Junior high school	L1 Korean/L2 English	To discuss hosting an American friend, etc.
Azkarai & García Mayo (2017)	Spain	Primary school	L1 Spanish/L2 English	To spot picture differences with a partner
Kobayashi & Kobayashi (2018)	Japan	University	L1 Japanese/L2 English	To present and discuss a self-created poster on a current topic

did, however, outperform exact repeaters on measures of syntactic complexity, and both groups improved their use of the simple past tense. Next, Azkarai and García Mayo (2017) investigated the two conditions of exact versus procedural repetition among children. When the task was repeated after three months, it was found that both groups made less use of their L1, and that its function shifted from phatic communication to coping with knowledge gaps. Repetition in Kobayashi and Kobayashi's (2018) study was operationalized as a poster carousel task during one lesson in which student groups presented a poster three times to different audiences. Students were shown to make adjustments to their subsequent performances based on backstage collaborative dialogue with other group members, instructor assistance, and appropriation of audience questions.

To make a few observations based on the growing task repetition literature:

- Monologic task repetition can benefit fluency, and these benefits may also extend to complexity and accuracy when careful online planning is implemented, such as in constant time conditions.
- Learners should be informed of the goal of repetition (e.g., improving multiple dimensions of speech production) so as to draw their attention to it during subsequent iterations.
- Interactive task repetition seems to yield benefits such as increased accuracy and decreased reliance on L1, though any differences between exact and procedural conditions remain somewhat unclear.
- Repeating tasks with different partners or audiences can help learners focus on their delivery and alleviate any potential boredom associated with repetition.
- More natural settings for repetition, such as the poster carousel task, offer many social learning affordances.

4.6 Evaluating the Research

TBLT research in educational settings can be conducted with an emphasis on task design or task implementation. If we remain open to both these possibilities, tasks appear to offer teachers both stability (complexity, mode) and flexibility (preparation, interaction, repetition). As stated at the beginning of the section, an interesting and enduring question for debate is whether the learning potential of tasks arises more from their fixed, abstract properties or from their varying, concrete particulars. Evidence from meta-analytic reviews shows that both contribute positively to learning outcomes, but currently reveals stronger effects for negotiated interaction than for task complexity (compare Keck et al., 2006 and

Jackson & Suethanapornkul, 2013), though it is premature to draw firm conclusions. Among the nuances to consider is the fact that complex tasks generate more interaction in the form of LREs (Révész, 2011; Kim, 2012 Kim & Taguchi, 2015). One can easily argue in favor of both efficient design and engaging implementation.

This review targeted recent studies on tasks in practice. Thus, these studies can be evaluated in terms of how well they meet the three criteria for establishing a researched pedagogy put forth by Samuda, Bygate, and Van den Branden (2018). These were *directionality* (from the classroom to language pedagogy), *transparency* (contextualization of task purpose/use in the actual educational setting), and *relevance* (to teaching in the form of pedagogic implications).

First, concerning their directionality, the studies were conducted in schools, often in classrooms, with learners collaborating alongside peers on tasks suited to their needs and interests. However, this selective review shows a slight bias toward university settings (fourteen of twenty-five studies, or 56 percent). It also reflects the predominance of English as a target language, despite some noteworthy exceptions (Kuiken & Vedder, 2011; Solon, Long, & Gurzynski-Weiss, 2017; Van de Guchte et al., 2019; see also Section 3 of this Element). From a classroom perspective, whether students speak various L1s or the same L1 is important. These conditions were represented by six versus nineteen of the studies reviewed, respectively. This is clear evidence that TBLT has been successfully adopted in same-L1, foreign language classrooms (Shehadeh & Coombe, 2012).

Second, regarding the issue of transparency, in each study, the task purpose was carefully described (see Tables 2–6). The authors did not merely theorize and specify workplans. They also discussed excerpts of learner production or interaction, highlighting the nature of the task-in-process. Nonetheless, it could also be argued that space limitations imposed by academic journals may, at times, discourage authors from offering detailed descriptions of the links between learner's needs, the tasks they research, and the wider curriculum context. Furthermore, the value of TBLT sometimes seems in danger of being obscured by technical discourse, which these studies contained.

Third, as for relevance, in many instances, the studies generated knowledge relevant to understanding teaching. They show that the research often targets areas of potentially overlapping interest to teachers and researchers (Spada, 2022). For instance, based on the bulleted summaries in each subsection in Section 4, instructors could develop ideas about how to plan sequences of tasks, guide performance using different modes, support learner preparation, match students for group and pair work, or repeat tasks. The work summarized offers practical insight drawn from a range of geographic locations and educational settings, with a focus on the needs of adult, and to a lesser extent, child L2 learners.

Thanks to an increasingly active research community, it is even truer now than when first asserted that "TBLT is the closest thing to a researched language pedagogy that exists" (Long, 2015, p. 343). Nevertheless, there is no guarantee that research on tasks will always be understandable and meaningful to educators. Furthermore, for all the information it provides, in the classroom, a thriving literature is no substitute for teacher expertise, gained through personal encounters with target and pedagogic tasks. TBLT research seems ideally positioned to achieve its aims when it is located in schools in which teachers and researchers are similarly invested, its realization is a process imbued with ethical values shared by local communities, and its findings represent a dialogue about what we want and need to know concerning language education in particular settings. Thus, close attention has also been paid to teachers and tasks.

5 Teachers and Tasks

The relationship between teachers and tasks is another steadily emerging area of interest and it is one of the most practical lines of TBLT research. As noted in the previous section, tasks provide teachers with flexibility and stability. However, one needs to be careful not to anthropomorphize tasks. In addition to the fact that teachers introduce tasks to their students, there is a broad and long-standing consensus that teachers play a role in fostering learner participation and guiding attention to meaning-making during implementation (e.g., Long & Robinson, 1998; Norris, 2009; Prabhu, 1987; Samuda, 2001; Willis, 1996; see Section 2.4 of this Element). More recently, they are additionally recognized as being agents of change in curricular innovation (Van den Branden, 2016; see Section 3.2 of this Element). This section provides further coverage of studies into teachers' experiences with understanding, preparing for, and doing TBLT.

5.1 Teacher Perspectives

A number of studies have considered how teachers responded to the introduction of tasks in various educational settings (e.g., McDonough & Chaikitmongkol, 2007). A study in Hong Kong revealed that, even with clear guidelines from education authorities, teachers raised issues concerning use of the L1, classroom management, and the amount and quality of students' L2 production (Carless, 2004; see also Chan, 2012). This resonates with findings from New Zealand where teachers faced with a new curriculum reported their lack of knowledge about TBLT, concerns about its effectiveness, and worries about preparing students for high-stakes examinations (East, 2012). Teachers in Ukrainian schools have likewise identified challenges to implementation, including compulsory marking, excessive noise, and time constraints (Bogachenko & Oliver, 2020). In the face of such challenges, and without additional training, teachers may opt for task-supported approaches that retain a strong focus on grammar and utilize tasks for communication practice, as has been reported in the Chinese context (Zheng & Borg, 2014; Chen & Wright, 2017). There are also reports of teachers lacking clarity regarding the definition of tasks (Erlam, 2016; Oliver & Bogachenko, 2018). In light of these studies, one can assume that moving from traditional practices to the optimal use of tasks will require further preparation and collaboration.

5.2 Teacher Preparation

A few studies have investigated whether integrating task-based principles into university courses taken by preservice teachers might predispose them toward the approach, with mixed results. Ogilvie and Dunn (2010) found that participants significantly improved in their disposition to TBLT from the beginning to the end of an L2 pedagogy course, although these individuals also noted reasons for not adopting tasks in a later practicum. Jackson (2012) illustrated how participants in a TESOL methods course gained practical knowledge from performing teaching tasks. However, there were no significant differences in attitudes toward TBLT between these participants and a group of nontrainee peers: both groups held positive attitudes. According to Chacón (2012), prospective teachers reported that being asked to carry out film-oriented tasks to improve their L2 ability gave them insight into how to use TBLT. A limitation of these studies is that they did not investigate the impact of these interventions over the long-term (but see East, in press, which presents a longer-term perspective on preservice teacher education and TBLT).

Research has also been undertaken with in-service teachers. These studies highlight the diversity of approaches to preparing teachers to create and/or use tasks. Such approaches have included short-term intensive training programs (Bryfonski, 2021), action research done in conjunction with task-based lessons (Zhu, 2020), courses and workshops using loop approaches wherein teachers experience and reflect on L2 tasks themselves (Hall, 2015; Sherris et al., 2013), exploratory practice to better understand the competencies supporting teacher-led focus on form (Müller-Hartmann & Schocker, 2018), and government-sponsored faculty development programs (Cozonac, 2004). In one detailed study, Bryfonski (2021, p. 16) reported "varied success in TBLT implementation after training" among first-year teachers assigned to English-Spanish bilingual schools in Honduras. Lessons prepared by these teachers used input elaboration, but were not highly individualized. Teachers viewed their lessons as promoting cooperative/collaborative learning, though not as providing negative feedback. In other words, these teachers partly succeeded in putting Long's (2015) methodological principles into practice. The author concluded by recommending that more attention be paid to teachers' prior experience and more time be spent on educating teachers about principles that seem challenging to implement.

5.3 Teacher Agency

Teacher involvement is crucial to TBLT, whether their role involves designing or implementing tasks. Studies of these two areas are invaluable for understanding teachers' readiness to engage in TBLT. First, a seminal study by Johnson (2003) investigated how expert versus novice materials designers went about creating a task from a design brief. The brief specified the learners' proficiency, hours of instruction, and a linguistic target and asked participants to prepare an interactive speaking lesson lasting fifteen to thirty minutes. Based on the results, Johnson hypothesized that good task designers possess many attributes, including visualization capacity, learner/context sensitivity, and a wide repertoire, among others. Several other studies, as well, have probed how teachers design and evaluate tasks for the classroom (Ellis, 2015; Erlam, 2016) as well as the extent to which they draw upon task complexity frameworks in planning lessons (Baralt, Harmath-de Lemos, & Werfelli, 2014). For instance, it has been found that in spite of teachers' positive opinions, individual and institutional factors mediate their adoption of lessons incorporating task complexity principles (Gurzynski-Weiss, 2016). Clearly, capacity, self-direction, and freedom from constraints, which are components of teacher autonomy (Jackson, 2018), are important in order for teachers to meaningfully act on knowledge gleaned from task-based research.

Second, moving beyond their potential role as designers, teachers are active agents when they use tasks. For instance, a recent study (Jackson, 2021) showed the advantages of putting preservice teachers in charge of tasks. In this study, sixteen participants in the teacher's role engaged in a series of map tasks with a partner in the student's role. As for the benefits, first, the teacher participants noticed verbal and nonverbal resources that facilitate task performance. Second, the use of video-based stimulated recall methodology allowed them to see how they managed the interactions, which were often successful. Third, the intervention encouraged the development of professional identities by inviting participants to act, think, and speak as teachers do (Jackson & Shirakawa, 2020). Engagement in tasks also benefits in-service teachers, as Samuda (2015) noted. She proposed that teachers construct a series of plans, spanning their lesson plan, their dynamic or in-class plans, and their retrospective plan, which can be used in future teaching. Based on these studies, effective instructors possess a sophisticated communicative repertoire, responsiveness to contingencies arising during tasks, and a forward-looking orientation to their role as teacher based on reflective practice. For a recent study with teachers that sought to bridge an in-service program with classroom implementation, see Erlam and Tolosa's (2022) work.

6 Epilogue: The Potential of TBLT

In this epilogue, three purposes for putting tasks into practice are described. The intent is to encapsulate to a degree the transformative potential of TBLT. Past work on it contains seeds for growth and change. The feasibility of these rationales for using tasks will naturally vary according to the context, the learners, and the teacher. Having thoroughly considered *what* tasks are and *how* they are used, this section provides answers to the question of *why* language educators, as key agents in its successful implementation, should continue to invest time and effort in curricular innovation guided by TBLT.

6.1 Transforming Classroom Learning

The aim of TBLT is to transform classrooms (whether face-to-face or virtual) into spaces full of rich, elaborated input and collaborative/cooperative interaction (Long, 2015). It sets out to establish a context for balanced L2 learning, viewed here as both acquisition and participation (Ortega, 2011). In response to the question of where the learning comes from in TBLT (Shehadeh, 2005), a partial list of processes associated with learning in such settings appears in Table 7. Apart from any explicit teaching – of questionable value because much of what language users know cannot be taught – learning derives from what students do in tasks, as "an active, personally conducted affair" (Dewey, 1916, p. 320).

On one hand, to acquire an L2, adults must *notice*, or attend to input with some level of awareness. Schmidt (1990, p. 149) argued that noticing plays

Table 7 Some fundamental processes in task-based classroom learning

Cognitive processes	Social processes
Noticing	Turn-taking
Chunking	Sequence organization
Categorization	Repair
Contingency learning	Recipient design

a role in task-based settings: "incidental learning is certainly possible when task demands focus attention on relevant features of the input.". Once noticing has taken place, a default implicit processing mode is assumed to operate (Long, 2015). Implicit learning ability, which involves the learning of patterns based upon multiple, recurring instances, has a very small, yet still positive relationship with L2 outcomes (Jackson & Maie, in press). According to usage-based accounts (Ellis, Römer & O'Donnell, 2016), associative mechanisms may further strengthen learning from noticed instances. These mechanisms include *chunking* language items, which leads to fluency, *categorization*, which aids the organization of linguistic units according to meaning, and learning of *contingencies* between different units, which drive prediction during L2 use. Such cognitive processes contribute to L2 proficiency and, therefore, task materials designed to engage them build learners' semantic knowledge.

On the other hand, to actively participate during tasks, learners must also attend to social processes. Tasks, whether inside or outside of the classroom, require cooperation among speakers to achieve a goal or aim. In settings of conversational language use, speakers use a number of processes to manage interaction, including *turn-taking* (how speakers begin and end turns appropriately), *sequence organization* (how adjacent turns build upon one another), *repair* (how speakers and listeners resolve miscommunication), and *recipient design* (how speakers design their utterances for specific hearers). These observable indicators of social interaction contribute to L2 competence (Pekarek Doehler & Pochon-Berger, 2015). A fuller account of participation across target and pedagogic tasks would go further to consider the relationships between language users, the choices inherent in spoken versus written language, and the influence of various resources, including technology, on meaning-making. In the classroom, having learners adopt specific roles during tasks builds their pragmatic knowledge.

Some of the processes in Table 7 were mentioned earlier (e.g., noticing, repair), whereas others constitute areas for future study. In short, tasks transform classrooms by creating contexts for primarily student-centered learning processes. This consequently alters the teacher's role, which emphasizes their *noticing* (Jackson, 2021) of learners' cognitive, behavioral, social, and emotional engagement (Philp & Duchesne, 2016). Teachers in task-based settings should try to notice and promote student involvement.

6.2 Transforming Language Programs

Whether the notion of task is expressed in technical terms (as a "unit of analysis", Long, 1985, p. 89), or educational terms (as a "pedagogic tool",

Samuda & Bygate, 2008, p. 60), its contribution to language programs can be substantial (Long & Norris, 2000; Markee, 1997; Norris, 2009, 2015). At this scale, TBLT cannot be understood without attention to complex social realities (Byrnes, 2019). The types of questions then raised can be partly illustrated by referring back to the curriculum framework introduced in Section 2:

1. Needs analysis – What sources and methods are used to determine needs? How do past, present, and future students inform program developers' understandings of relevant target tasks?
2. Task selection and sequencing – In what way(s) are pedagogic tasks organized across the curriculum and within courses? To what extent does their arrangement promote ongoing learner development?
3. Materials development – Does the program rely on in-house or commercial materials and are these resources task-based? Which materials may benefit from further development?
4. Teaching – What qualifications, expertise, and support are needed for teachers to engage in task-based instruction? How are teachers made aware of the program's alignment with TBLT?
5. Assessment – What roles do formative and summative assessment play? Does the program utilize task-based language assessment and, if so, how does it communicate its outcomes?
6. Evaluation – How, by whom, and for what purposes is each of the aforementioned components evaluated? And how might evaluation improve the program overall?

If TBLT is to transform language programs, then those in charge of its implementation will need to think through these and many other questions. Despite the enormity of this undertaking, programmatic thinking is valuable because it fosters understanding of classroom realities, longitudinal development, contextual factors, and, ultimately, the potential of task-based programs and their graduates (Norris, 2015).

6.3 Transforming Societies

Recently, Crookes and Ziegler (2021) considered the compatibility between TBLT, as a mainstream approach to language education based on SLA research, and critical language pedagogy, which is grounded in social justice. They pointed out several areas of potential overlap, among them the use of critical needs analysis to uncover problematic issues in learners' lives. Through task-based dialogue, students can be awakened to forms of oppression including bullying at school (Konoeda & Watanabe, 2008) and media stereotypes (da Silva, 2020). The affinity between task-based and critical perspectives also extends to teacher education, as described by Vieira (2017), whose study of two beginning teachers revealed how tasks enabled them to promote student choice, authentic language use, and engagement with issues, including democratic participation. She described the use of tasks by these teachers as providing space "between reality and ideals", where "possibilities for transformation are explored" (Vieira, 2017, p. 711).

Seeking to align TBLT with critical language pedagogy links it to democracy and raises questions of when and how it might enact those principles (Crookes, 2021). From this perspective, one might ask whether a given implementation of tasks reflects the following democratic values:

- Choice – To what extent are learners involved in decisions related to individual tasks or even the overall curriculum and its implementation? Do any choices presented to them faithfully represent their concerns and interests?
- Equality – Does classroom discourse put teachers and all learners on equal footing? Do materials and teaching invite discussion of inequalities due to race, gender, religion, sexual orientation, and social class?
- Solidarity – Do teachers, learners, and other participants form bonds through collaboration? Does the use of tasks promote intercultural awareness and acceptance?

Successful TBLT might address needs less fundamental than those expressed above. Nonetheless, unlike some language teaching approaches, TBLT can nurture an environment conducive to them, if carried out with an understanding of – and a commitment to – its learner-centered and communicative nature. By reshaping classrooms to promote balanced L2 development and reorienting programs to major challenges in the real world, TBLT may ultimately contribute to empowering students and transforming society for the better.

Appendix: Discussion Questions

1. A jigsaw puzzle can be done by one person whereas a jigsaw task cannot. State in your own words why this is so and give an example of any task type in Section 1.4.

2. Which of the six curricular components in Section 2 seems the most and least challenging to develop? Give reasons for your answers.

3. What social or cultural factors might arise when seeking to implement tasks? Start by listing any of those mentioned in Section 3, then add your own ideas.

4. Does the effectiveness of pedagogic tasks depend mostly on careful design or skillful implementation? Support your answer with evidence from Section 4.

5. In light of Section 5, what knowledge, skills, and attitudes might help teachers put tasks into practice?

6. Describe one problematic issue faced by society. How might critical TBLT (Section 6.3) help to raise learners' awareness of this issue?

7. How would you choose, design, and implement a task for a group of language learners?

References

Adams, R., Alwi, N. A. N. M., & Newton, J. (2015). Task complexity effects on the complexity and accuracy of writing via text chat. *Journal of Second Language Writing, 29,* 64–81. https://doi.org/10.1016/j.jslw.2015.06.002.

Ahmadian, M. J., & García Mayo, M. D. P. (Eds.). (2018). *Recent Perspectives on Task-Based Language Learning and Teaching.* Berlin: De Gruyter.

Ahmadian, M. J., & Tavakoli, M. (2011). The effects of simultaneous use of careful online planning and task repetition on accuracy, complexity, and fluency in EFL learners' oral production. *Language Teaching Research, 15*(1), 35–59. https://doi.org/10.1177/1362168810383329.

Anderson, J. (2019). Deconstructing jigsaw activities. *Modern English Teacher, 28*(2), 35–37. www.modernenglishteacher.com/deconstructing-jigsaw-activities

Anderson, N., & McCutcheon, N. (2019). *Activities for Task-Based Learning: Integrating a Fluency First Approach into the ELT Classroom.* Stuttgart: Delta.

Aubrey, S. (2017). Measuring flow in the EFL classroom: Learners' perceptions of inter- and intra-cultural task-based interactions. *TESOL Quarterly, 51*(3), 661–692. https://doi.org/10.1002/tesq.387.

Azkarai, A., & García Mayo, M. D. P. (2017). Task repetition effects on L1 use in EFL child task-based interaction. *Language Teaching Research, 21*(4), 480–495. https://doi.org/10.1177/1362168816654169.

Baralt, M., Gilabert, R., & Robinson, P. (2014). *Task Sequencing and Instructed Second Language Learning.* London: Bloomsbury.

Baralt, M., Gurzynski-Weiss, L., & Kim, Y. (2016). Engagement with the language: How examining learners' affective and social engagement explains successful learner-generated attention to form. In M. Sato & S. Ballinger (Eds.), *Peer Interaction and Second Language Learning: Pedagogical Potential and Research Agenda* (pp. 209–239). Amsterdam: John Benjamins.

Baralt, M., Harmath-de Lemos, S., & Werfelli, S. (2014). Teachers' application of the Cognition Hypothesis when lesson planning: A case study. In M. Baralt, R. Gilabert, & P. Robinson (Eds.), *Task Sequencing and Instructed Second Language Learning* (pp. 179–206). London: Bloomsbury.

Behney, J., & Gass, S. (2021). *Interaction.* Cambridge: Cambridge University Press.

Benevides, M., & Valvona, C. (2018). *Widgets Inc.: A Task-Based Course in Workplace English* (2nd ed.). Tokyo: Atama-ii.

Blake, R. (2000). Computer mediated communication: A window on L2 Spanish interlanguage. *Language Learning & Technology, 4*(1), 111–125. http://dx.doi.org/10125/25089.

Bogachenko, T., & Oliver, R. (2020). The potential use of tasks in post-Soviet schools: Case studies from Ukraine. In C. Lambert & R. Oliver (Eds.), *Using Tasks in Second Language Teaching: Practice in Diverse Contexts* (pp. 162–177). Bristol: Multilingual Matters.

Borro, I. (2022). Comparing the effectiveness of task-based language teaching and presentation-practice-production on second language grammar learning. In M. J. Ahmadian & M. H. Long (Eds.), *The Cambridge Handbook of Task-Based Language Teaching* (pp. 549–565). Cambridge: Cambridge University Press.

Breen, M. P. (1987). Learner contributions to task design. In C. Candlin & E. Murphy (Eds.), *Language Learning Tasks* (pp. 23–46). London: Prentice Hall.

Breen, M. P., & Littlejohn, A. (2000). The significance of negotiation. In M. P. Breen & A. Littlejohn (Eds.), *Classroom Decision-Making: Negotiation and Process Syllabuses in Practice* (pp. 5–38). Cambridge: Cambridge University Press.

Brindley, G. (1994). Task-centered language assessment in language learning: The promise and the challenge. In N. Bird, P. Falvey, A. Tsui, D. Allison, & A. McNeill (Eds.), *Language and Learning: Papers Presented at the Annual International Language in Education Conference, Hong Kong* (pp. 73–94). Hong Kong: Hong Kong Education Department.

Brown, J. D. (1995). *The Elements of Language Curriculum: A Systematic Approach to Program Development*. Boston: Heinle & Heinle.

Brown, J. D., Hudson, T., Norris, J., & Bonk, W. J. (2002). *An Investigation of Second Language Task-Based Performance Assessments*. Honolulu: University of Hawai'i, Second Language Teaching & Curriculum Center.

Bryfonski, L. (2021). From task-based training to task-based instruction: Novice language teachers' experiences and perspectives. *Language Teaching Research*. https://doi.org/10.1177/13621688211026570.

Bryfonski, L., & McKay, T. H. (2019). TBLT implementation and evaluation: A meta-analysis. *Language Teaching Research, 23*(5), 603–632. https://doi.org/10.1177/1362168817744389.

Bui, H. Y. G. (2014). Task readiness: Theoretical framework and empirical evidence from topic familiarity, strategic planning, and proficiency levels.

In P. Skehan (Ed.), *Processing Perspectives on Task Performance* (pp. 63–93). Amsterdam: John Benjamins.

Butler, Y. G. (2011). The implementation of communicative and task-based language teaching in the Asia-Pacific region. *Annual Review of Applied Linguistics, 31*, 36–57. https://doi.org/10.1017/S0267190511000122.

Bygate, M. (2000). Introduction. *Language Teaching Research, 4*(3), 185–192. https://doi.org/10.1177/136216880000400301.

Bygate, M. (2018). Introduction. In M. Bygate (Ed.), *Learning Language through Task Repetition* (pp. 1–25). Amsterdam: John Benjamins.

Bygate, M., Skehan, P., & Swain, M. (2001). Introduction. In M. Bygate, P. Skehan, & M. Swain (Eds.), *Researching Pedagogic Tasks: Second Language Learning, Teaching and Testing* (pp. 1–20). Harlow: Pearson Education Limited.

Byrnes, H. (2014). Linking task and writing for language development: Evidence from a genre-based curricular approach. In H. Byrnes & R. M. Manchón (Eds.), *Task-Based Language Learning – Insights from and for L2 Writing* (pp. 237–263). Amsterdam: John Benjamins.

Byrnes, H. (2015). Linking "task" and curricular thinking. In M. Bygate (Ed.), *Domains and Directions in the Development of TBLT: A Decade of Plenaries from the International Conference* (pp. 193–224). Amsterdam: John Benjamins.

Byrnes, H. (2019). Affirming the context of instructed SLA: The potential of curricular thinking. *Language Teaching Research, 23*(4), 514–532. https://doi.org/10.1177/1362168818776666.

Byrnes, H., & Manchón, R. M. (2014). Task-based language learning: Insights from and for L2 writing: An introduction. In H. Byrnes & R. M. Manchón (Eds.), *Task-Based Language Learning – Insights from and for L2 Writing* (pp. 1–27). Amsterdam: John Benjamins.

Byrnes, H., Maxim, H. H., & Norris, J. M. (2010). Realizing advanced foreign language writing development in collegiate education: Curricular design, pedagogy, assessment [Special issue]. *The Modern Language Journal, 94*(s1). https://doi.org/10.1111/j.1540-4781.2010.01147.x.

Byrnes, H., Crane, C., Maxim, H. H., & Sprang, K. A. (2006). Taking text to task: Issues and choices in curriculum construction. *ITL: International Journal of Applied Linguistics, 152*(1), 85–110. https://doi.org/10.2143/ITL.152.0.2017864.

Candlin, C. N. (1987). Towards task-based language learning. In C. N. Candlin & D. Murphy (Eds.), *Language Learning Tasks* (pp. 5–22). London: Prentice Hall.

Carless, D. (2004). Issues in teachers' reinterpretation of a task-based innovation in primary schools. *TESOL Quarterly, 38*(4), 639–662. https://doi.org/10.2307/3588283.

Chacón, C. T. (2012). Task-based language teaching through film-oriented activities in a teacher education program in Venezuela. In A. Shehadeh & C. A. Coombe (Eds.), *Task-Based Language Teaching in Foreign Language Contexts: Research and Implementation* (pp. 241–266). Amsterdam: John Benjamins.

Chan, S. P. S. (2012). Qualitative differences in novice teachers' enactment of task-based language teaching in Hong Kong primary classrooms. In A. Shehadeh & C. A. Coombe (Eds.), *Task-Based Language Teaching in Foreign Language Contexts: Research and Implementation* (pp. 187–214). Amsterdam: John Benjamins.

Chen, Q., & Wright, C. (2017). Contextualization and authenticity in TBLT: Voices from Chinese classrooms. *Language Teaching Research, 21*(4), 517–538. https://doi.org/10.1177/1362168816639985.

Chow, A., & Li, B. (2008). Task-based assessment. In A. Ma (Ed.), *A Practical Guide to a Task-Based Curriculum: Planning, Grammar Teaching, and Assessment* (pp. 101–178). Hong Kong: City University of Hong Kong Press.

Cozonac, K. (2004). It's all in the team: Approaches to teacher development in a content-based, task-based EFL program. In B. L. Leaver & J. R. Willis (Eds.), *Task-Based Instruction in Foreign Language Education: Practices and Programs* (pp. 280–295). Washington, DC: Georgetown.

Crookes, G. V. (2021). Critical language pedagogy: An introduction to principles and values. *ELT Journal, 75*(3), 247–255. https://doi.org/10.1093/elt/ccab020.

Crookes, G. V., & Ziegler, N. (2021). Critical language pedagogy and task-based language teaching: Reciprocal relationship and mutual benefit. *Education Sciences, 11*(6), 1–19. https://doi.org/10.3390/educsci11060254.

da Silva, L. (2020). Critical tasks in action: The role of the teacher in the implementation of tasks designed from a critical perspective. *Ilha do Desterro, 73*(1), 109–127. https://doi.org/10.5007/2175-8026.2020v73n1p109.

Dao, P., & McDonough, K. (2017). The effect of task role on Vietnamese EFL learners' collaboration in mixed proficiency dyads. *System, 65*, 15–24. https://doi.org/10.1016/j.system.2016.12.012.

Dewey, J. (1916). *Democracy and Education*. Mineola: Dover.

Dörnyei, Z. (2002). The motivational basis of language learning tasks. In P. Robinson (Ed.), *Individual Differences and Instructed Language Learning* (pp. 137–158). Amsterdam: John Benjamins.

Doughty, C. J., & Long, M. H. (2003). Optimal psycholinguistic environments for distance foreign language learning. *Language Learning & Technology*, *7*(3), 50–80. http://dx.doi.org/10125/25214.

Duff, P. A. (1986). Another look at interlanguage talk: Taking task to task. In R. R. Day (Ed.), *Talking to Learn: Conversation in Second Language Acquisition* (pp. 147–181). Rowley: Newbury House.

East, M. (2012). *Task-Based Language Teaching from the Teachers' Perspective*. Amsterdam: John Benjamins.

East, M. (2021). *Foundational Principles of Task-Based Language Teaching*. New York: Routledge.

East, M. (In press). *Mediating Innovation through Language Teacher Education*. Cambridge: Cambridge University Press.

Ellis, N. C., Römer, U., & O'Donnell, M. B. (2016). *Usage-Based Approaches to Language Acquisition and Processing: Cognitive and Corpus Investigations of Construction Grammar*. Malden, MA: Wiley-Blackwell.

Ellis, R. (2005). Planning and task-based performance: Theory and research. In R. Ellis (Ed.). *Planning and Task Performance in a Second Language* (pp. 3–34). Amsterdam: John Benjamins.

Ellis, R. (2015). Teachers evaluating tasks. In M. Bygate (Ed.), *Domains and Directions in the Development of TBLT: A Decade of Plenaries from the International Conference* (pp. 247–270). Amsterdam: John Benjamins.

Ellis, R. (2018). *Reflections on Task-Based Language Teaching*. Bristol: Multilingual Matters.

Ellis, R., Skehan, P., Li, S., Shintani, N., & Lambert, C. (2019). *Task-Based Language Teaching: Theory and Practice*. Cambridge: Cambridge University Press.

Erlam, R. (2016). "I'm still not sure what a task is": Teachers designing language tasks. *Language Teaching Research*, *20*(3), 279–299. https://doi.org/10.1177/1362168814566087.

Erlam, R., & Tolosa, C. (2022). *Pedagogical Realities of Implementing Task-Based Language Teaching*. Amsterdam: John Benjamins.

Fujii, A., Ziegler, N., & Mackey, A. (2016). Peer interaction and metacognitive instruction in the EFL classroom. In M. Sato & S. Ballinger (Eds.), *Peer Interaction and Second Language Learning: Pedagogical Potential and Research Agenda* (pp. 63–89). Amsterdam: John Benjamins.

González-Lloret, M. (2014). The need for needs analysis in technology-mediated TBLT. In M. González-Lloret & L. Ortega (Eds.), *Technology-Mediated TBLT: Researching Technology and Tasks* (pp. 23–50). Amsterdam: John Benjamins.

González-Lloret, M. (2016). *A Practical Guide to Integrating Technology into Task-Based Language Teaching*. Washington, DC: Georgetown.

González-Lloret, M., & Nielson, K. B. (2015). Evaluating TBLT: The case of a task-based Spanish program. *Language Teaching Research, 19*(5), 525–549. https://doi.org/10.1177/1362168814541745.

González-Lloret, M., & Ortega, L. (Eds.) (2014a). *Technology-Mediated TBLT: Researching Technology and Tasks*. Amsterdam: John Benjamins.

González-Lloret, M., & Ortega, L. (2014b). Towards technology-mediated TBLT: An introduction. In M. González-Lloret & L. Ortega (Eds.), *Technology-Mediated TBLT: Researching Technology and Tasks* (pp. 1–21). Amsterdam: John Benjamins.

Hall, S. J. (2015). Gaining acceptance of task-based teaching during Malaysian rural in-service teacher training. In Thomas, M. & Reinders, H. (Eds.), *Contemporary Task-Based Teaching in Asia* (pp. 156–169). London: Bloomsbury.

Harris, J., & Leeming, P. (2018). *On Task 1*. Tokyo: ABAX ELT Publishers.

Hill, Y. Z., & Tschudi, S. L. (2011). Exploring task-based curriculum development in a blended-learning conversational Chinese program. *International Journal of Virtual and Personal Learning Environments, 2*(1), 19–36. https://doi.org/10.4018/jvple.2011010102.

Gilabert, R., & Barón, J. (2018). Independently measuring cognitive complexity in task design for interlanguage pragmatics development. In N. Taguchi & Y. Kim (Eds.), *Task-Based Approaches to Teaching and Assessing Pragmatics* (pp. 159–190). Amsterdam: John Benjamins.

Gilabert, R., Manchón, R., & Vasylets, O. (2016). Mode in theoretical and empirical TBLT research: Advancing research agendas. *Annual Review of Applied Linguistics, 36*, 117–135. https://doi.org/10.1017/S0267190515000112.

Gokool, R., & Visser, M. (2021). IsiZulu task-based syllabus for medical students: Grading and sequencing doctor-patient communication tasks. *South African Journal of African Languages, 41*(2), 149–159. https://doi.org/10.1080/02572117.2021.1948214.

Gurzynski-Weiss, L. (2016). Spanish instructors' operationalization of task complexity and task sequencing in foreign language lessons. *The Language Learning Journal, 44*(4), 467–486. https://doi.org/10.1080/09571736.2015.1015151.

Gurzynski-Weiss, L. (2017). L2 instructor individual characteristics. In S. Loewen & M. Sato (Eds.), *The Routledge Handbook of Instructed Second Language Acquisition* (pp. 451–467). New York: Routledge.

Gurzynski-Weiss, L. (2021). Let's talk tasks: A conversation between task-based researchers, language teachers, and teacher trainers. *TASK, 1*(1), 138–149. https://doi.org/10.1075/task.00012.gur.

Gurzynski-Weiss, L., & IATBLT (n.d.). The TBLT Language Learning Task Bank. https://tblt.indiana.edu

Jackson, D. O. (2011). Convergent and divergent computer-mediated communication tasks in an English for academic purposes course. *TESL-EJ, 15*(3), 1–18. http://tesl-ej.org/pdf/ej59/a1.pdf.

Jackson, D. O. (2012). Task-based language teacher education in an undergraduate program in Japan. In A. Shehadeh & C. A. Coombe (Eds.), *Task-Based Language Teaching in Foreign Language Contexts: Research and Implementation* (pp. 267–285). Amsterdam: John Benjamins.

Jackson, D. O. (2018). Teacher autonomy. In J. Liontas & M. DelliCarpini (Eds.), *TESOL Encyclopedia of English Language Teaching* (pp. 1–6). Hoboken: Wiley.

Jackson, D. O. (2021). *Language Teacher Noticing in Tasks*. Bristol: Multilingual Matters.

Jackson, D. O., & Burch, A. R. (2017). Complementary theoretical perspectives on task-based classroom realities. *TESOL Quarterly, 51*(3), 493–506. https://doi.org/10.1002/tesq.393.

Jackson, D. O., & Maie, R. (In press). Implicit statistical learning and second language outcomes: A Bayesian meta-analysis. In Z. E. Wen, P. Skehan, & R. Sparks (Eds.), *Language Aptitude Theory and Practice*. Cambridge: Cambridge University Press.

Jackson, D. O., & Shirakawa, T. (2020). Identity, noticing, and emotion among pre-service English language teachers. In B. Yazan & K. Lindahl (Eds.), *Language Teacher Identity in TESOL: Teacher Education and Practice as Identity Work* (pp. 197–212). New York: Routledge.

Jackson, D. O., & Suethanapornkul, S. (2013). The Cognition Hypothesis: A synthesis and meta-analysis of research on second language task complexity. *Language Learning, 63*(2), 330–367. https://doi.org/10.1111/lang.12008.

Johnson, K. (2003). *Designing Language Teaching Tasks*. New York: Palgrave.

Johnson, M. D. (2017). Cognitive task complexity and L2 written syntactic complexity, accuracy, lexical complexity, and fluency: A research synthesis and meta-analysis. *Journal of Second Language Writing, 37*, 13–38. https://doi.org/10.1016/j.jslw.2017.06.001.

Kang, S., & Lee, J. H. (2019). Are two heads always better than one? The effects of collaborative planning on L2 writing in relation to task complexity. *Journal of Second Language Writing, 45*, 61–72. https://doi.org/10.1016/j.jslw.2019.08.001.

Kato, Y., Matsumura, M., Wicking, P., et al. (2020). *Komyunikēshon tasuku no aidea to materiaru: Kyōshitsu to sekai o tsunagu eigo jugyō no tame ni [Ideas and Materials for Communication through Tasks: Connecting the English Language Classroom with the Real World*]. Tokyo: Sanshusha.

Keck, C. M., Iberri-Shea, G., Tracy-Ventura, N., & Wa-Mbaleka, S. (2006). Investigating the empirical link between task-based interaction and acquisition: A meta-analysis. In J. M. Norris & L. Ortega (Eds.), *Synthesizing Research on Language Learning and Teaching* (pp. 91–131). Amsterdam: John Benjamins.

Kim, Y. (2012). Task complexity, learning opportunities, and Korean EFL learners' question development. *Studies in Second Language Acquisition*, *34*(4), 627–658. https://doi.org/10.1017/S0272263112000368.

Kim, Y., & Taguchi, N. (2015). Promoting task-based pragmatics instruction in EFL classroom contexts: The role of task complexity. *The Modern Language Journal*, *99*(4), 656–677. https://doi.org/10.1111/modl.12273.

Kim, Y., & Tracy-Ventura, N. (2013). The role of task repetition in L2 performance development: What needs to be repeated during task-based interaction? *System*, *41*(3), 829–840. https://doi.org/10.1016/j.system.2013.08.005.

Kobayashi, E., & Kobayashi, M. (2018). Second language learning through repeated engagement in a poster presentation task. In M. Bygate (Ed.), *Learning Language through Task Repetition* (pp. 223–254). Amsterdam: John Benjamins.

Konoeda, K., & Watanabe, Y. (2008). Task-based critical pedagogy in Japanese EFL classrooms: Rationale, principles, and examples. In M. Mantero, P. C. Miller, & J. L. Watzke (Eds.), *Readings in Language Studies: Language across Disciplinary Boundaries* (pp. 45–72). St. Louis: International Society for Language Studies.

Kormos, J. (2014). Differences across modalities of performance: An investigation of linguistic and discourse complexity in narrative tasks. In H. Byrnes & R. M. Manchón (Eds.), *Task-Based Language Learning – Insights from and for L2 Writing* (pp. 193–216). Amsterdam: John Benjamins.

Kuiken, F., & Vedder, I. (2011). Task complexity and linguistic performance in L2 writing and speaking: The effect of mode. In P. Robinson (Ed.), *x Task Complexity: Researching the Cognition Hypothesis of Language Learning and Performance* (pp. 91–104). Amsterdam: John Benjamins.

Kunitz, S., & Skogmyr Marian, K. (2017). Tracking immanent language learning behavior over time in task-based classroom work. *TESOL Quarterly*, *51*(3), 507–535. https://doi.org/10.1002/tesq.389.

Lambert, C., Philp, J., & Nakamura, S. (2017). Learner-generated content and engagement in second language task performance. *Language Teaching Research*, *21*(6), 665–680. https://doi.org/10.1177/1362168816683559.

Larsen-Freeman, D. (2018). Task repetition or task iteration? It does make a difference. In M. Bygate (Ed.), *Learning Language through Task Repetition* (pp. 311–329). Amsterdam: John Benjamins.

Le, H. T. (2021). Exploring L2 learners' task-related identities in a reading circle task through conversation analysis. *Canadian Journal of Applied Linguistics, 24*(2), 128–155. https://doi.org/10.37213/cjal.2021.31343.

Lee, J., & Burch, A. R. (2017). Collaborative planning in process: An ethnomethodological perspective. *TESOL Quarterly, 51*(3), 536–575. https://doi.org/10.1002/tesq.386.

Loschky, L., & Bley-Vroman, R. (1993). Grammar and task-based methodology. In S. Crookes & S. M. Gass (Eds.), *Tasks and Language Learning: Integrating Theory and Practice* (pp. 123–167). Clevedon: Multilingual Matters.

Long, M. H. (1985). A role for instruction in second language acquisition: Task-based language teaching. In K. Hyltenstam & M. Pienemann (Eds.), *Modelling and Assessing Second Language Acquisition* (pp. 77–99). Clevedon: Multilingual Matters.

Long, M. H. (1996). The role of the linguistic environment in second language acquisition. In W. C. Ritchie & T. K. Bhatia (Eds.), *Handbook of Second Language Acquisition* (pp. 413–468). New York: Academic Press.

Long, M. H. (Ed.). (2005). *Second Language Needs Analysis*. Cambridge: Cambridge University Press.

Long, M. H. (2015). *Second Language Acquisition and Task-Based Language Teaching*. Malden, MA: Wiley-Blackwell.

Long, M. H., & Ahmadian, M. J. (2022). Preface: The origins and growth of task-based language teaching. In M. J. Ahmadian & M. H. Long (Eds.), *The Cambridge Handbook of Task-Based Language Teaching* (pp. xxv–xxxii). Cambridge: Cambridge University Press.

Long, M., & Crookes, G. (1992). Three approaches to task-based syllabus design. *TESOL Quarterly, 26*(1), 27–56. https://doi.org/10.2307/3587368.

Long, M. H., & Norris, J. M. (2000). Task-based teaching and assessment. In M. Byram (Ed.), *Routledge Encyclopedia of Language Teaching and Learning* (pp. 597–603). London: Routledge.

Long, M. H., & Robinson, P. (1998). Focus on form: Theory, research, and practice. In C. Doughty & J. Williams (Eds.), *Focus on Form in Classroom Second Language Acquisition* (pp. 15–41). Cambridge: Cambridge University Press.

Mackey, A. (Ed.). (2007). *Conversational Interaction in Second Language Acquisition*. Oxford: Oxford University Press.

Mackey, A. (2012). *Input, Interaction, and Corrective Feedback in L2 Learning*. Oxford: Oxford University Press.

Mackey, A. (2020). *Interaction, Feedback and Task Research in Second Language Learning: Methods and Design*. Cambridge: Cambridge University Press.

Malicka, A. (2014). The role of task sequencing in monologic oral production. In M. Baralt, R. Gilabert, & Robinson, P. (Eds.), *Task Sequencing and Instructed Second Language Learning* (pp. 71–93). London: Bloomsbury.

Malicka, A., Gilabert Guerrero, R., & Norris, J. M. (2019). From needs analysis to task design: Insights from an English for specific purposes context. *Language Teaching Research, 23*(1), 78–106. https://doi.org/10.1177/1362168817714278.

Markee, N. (1997). *Managing Curricular Innovation*. Cambridge: Cambridge University Press.

McDonough, K. (2015). Perceived benefits and challenges with the use of collaborative tasks in EFL contexts. In M. Bygate (Ed.), *Domains and Directions in the Development of TBLT: A Decade of Plenaries from the International Conference* (pp. 225–246). Amsterdam: John Benjamins.

McDonough, K., & Chaikitmongkol, W. (2007). Teachers' and learners' reactions to a task-based EFL course in Thailand. *TESOL Quarterly, 41*(1), 107–132. https://doi.org/10.1002/j.1545-7249.2007.tb00042.x.

Michel, M. C. (2011). Effects of task complexity and interaction on L2 performance. In P. Robinson (Ed.), *Second Language Task Complexity: Researching the Cognition Hypothesis of Language Learning and Performance* (pp. 141–173). Amsterdam: John Benjamins.

Mochizuki, N., & Ortega, L. (2008). Balancing communication and grammar in beginning-level foreign language classrooms: A study of guided planning and relativization. *Language Teaching Research, 12*(1), 11–37. https://doi.org/10.1177/1362168807084492.

Müller-Hartmann, A., & Schocker, M. (2018). The challenges of integrating focus on form within tasks: Findings from a classroom research project in secondary EFL classrooms. In V. Samuda, K. Van den Branden, & M. Bygate (Eds.), *TBLT as a Researched Pedagogy* (pp. 97–129). Amsterdam: John Benjamins.

Müller-Hartmann, A., & Schocker-von Ditfurth. M. (2011). *Teaching English: Task-Supported Language Learning*. Paderborn: Schöningh.

Nakamura, S., Phung, L., & Reinders, H. (2021). The effect of learner choice on L2 task engagement. *Studies in Second Language Acquisition, 43*(2), 428–441. https://doi.org/10.1017/S027226312000042X.

Newton, J. (2022). The adoption of task-based language teaching in diverse contexts: Challenges and opportunities. In M. J. Ahmadian & M. H. Long

(Eds.), *The Cambridge Handbook of Task-Based Language Teaching* (pp. 639–670). Cambridge: Cambridge University Press.

Newton, J., & Bui, T. (2018). Teaching with tasks in primary school EFL classrooms in Vietnam. In M. J. Ahmadian & M. D. P. García Mayo (Eds.), *Recent Perspectives on Task-Based Language Learning and Teaching* (pp. 259–278). Berlin: De Gruyter.

Norris, J. M. (2009). Task-based teaching and testing. In M. H. Long & C. J. Doughty (Eds.), *The Handbook of Language Teaching* (pp. 578–594). Malden, MA: Wiley-Blackwell.

Norris, J. M. (2015). Thinking and acting programmatically in task-based language teaching. In M. Bygate (Ed.), *Domains and Directions in the Development of TBLT: A Decade of Plenaries from the International Conference* (pp. 27–57). Amsterdam: John Benjamins.

Norris, J. M. (2016). Current uses for task-based language assessment. *Annual Review of Applied Linguistics*, *36*, 230–244. https://doi.org/10.1017/S0267190516000027.

Norris, J. M., & Davis, J. M. (2022). Evaluating task-based language programs. In M. J. Ahmadian & M. H. Long (Eds.), *The Cambridge Handbook of Task-Based Language Teaching* (pp. 529–548). Cambridge: Cambridge University Press.

Norris, J. M., & East, M. (2022). Task-based language assessment. In M. J. Ahmadian & M. H. Long (Eds.), *The Cambridge Handbook of Task-Based Language Teaching* (pp. 507–28). Cambridge: Cambridge University Press.

Norris, J. M., Brown, J. D., Hudson, T., & Yoshioka, J. (1998). *Designing Second Language Performance Assessments*. Honolulu: University of Hawai'i, Second Language Teaching & Curriculum Center.

Nunan, D. (1989). *Designing Tasks for the Communicative Classroom*. Cambridge: Cambridge University Press.

Ogilvie, G., & Dunn, W. (2010). Taking teacher education to task: Exploring the role of teacher education in promoting the utilization of task-based language teaching. *Language Teaching Research*, *14*(2), 161–181. https://doi.org/10.1177/1362168809353875.

Oliver, R. (2020). Developing authentic tasks for the workplace using needs analysis: A case study of Australian Aboriginal vocational students. In C. Lambert & R. Oliver (Eds.), *Using Tasks in Second Language Teaching: Practice in Diverse Contexts* (pp. 146–61). Bristol: Multilingual Matters.

Oliver, R., & Bogachenko, T. (2018). Teacher perceptions and use of tasks in school ESL classrooms. In V. Samuda, K. Van den Branden, & M. Bygate

(Eds.), *TBLT as a Researched Pedagogy* (pp. 71–95). Amsterdam: John Benjamins.

Oliver, R., Philp, J., & Duchesne, S. (2017). Children working it out together: A comparison of younger and older learners collaborating in task-based interaction. *System*, *69*, 1–14. https://doi.org/10.1016/j.system.2017.08.001.

Ortega, L. (2007). Meaningful L2 practice in foreign language classrooms: A cognitive-interactionist SLA perspective. In R. M. DeKeyser (Ed.), *Practice in a Second Language: Perspectives from Applied Linguistics and Cognitive Psychology* (pp. 180–207). Cambridge: Cambridge University Press.

Ortega, L. (2011). SLA after the social turn: Where cognitivism and its alternatives stand. In D. Atkinson (Ed.), *Alternative Approaches to Second Language Acquisition* (pp. 167–180). Hoboken: Routledge.

Park, M. (2015). A needs analysis for a Korean middle school EFL general English curriculum. In M. Thomas & H. Reinders (Eds.), *Contemporary Task-Based Language Teaching in Asia* (pp. 261–278). London: Bloomsbury.

Pekarek Doehler, S., & Pochon-Berger, E. (2015). The development of L2 interactional competence: Evidence from turn-taking organization, sequence organization, repair organization, and preference organization. In T. Cadierno. & S. W. Eskildsen (Eds.), *Usage-Based Perspectives on Second Language Learning* (pp. 233–268). Berlin: De Gruyter.

Philp, J., & Duchesne, S. (2016). Exploring engagement in tasks in the language classroom. *Annual Review of Applied Linguistics*, *36*, 50–72. https://doi.org/10.1017/S0267190515000094.

Philp, J., Adams, R., & Iwashita, N. (2013). *Peer Interaction and Second Language Learning*. New York: Routledge.

Phung, L., Nakamura, S., & Reinders, H. (2021). The effect of choice on affective engagement: Implications for task design. In P. Hiver, A. H. Al-Hoorie, & S. Mercer (Eds.), *Student Engagement in the Language Classroom* (pp. 163–181). Bristol: Multilingual Matters.

Pica, T. (1994). Research on negotiation: What does it reveal about second-language learning conditions, processes, and outcomes? *Language Learning*, *44*(3), 493–527. https://doi.org/10.1111/j.1467-1770.1994.tb01115.x.

Pica, T., Kanagy, R., & Falodun, J. (1993). Choosing and using communication tasks for second language instruction and research. In S. Crookes & S. M. Gass (Eds.), *Tasks and Language Learning: Integrating Theory and Practice* (pp. 9–34). Clevedon: Multilingual Matters.

Pica, T., Kang, H. S., & Sauro, S. (2006). Information gap tasks: Their multiple roles and contributions to interaction research methodology.

Studies in Second Language Acquisition, 28(2), 301–338. https://doi.org/10.1017/S027226310606013X.

Prabhu, N. S. (1987). *Second Language Pedagogy.* Oxford: Oxford University Press.

Révész, A. (2011). Task complexity, focus on L2 constructions, and individual differences: A classroom-based study. *The Modern Language Journal, 95,* 162–181. https://doi.org/10.1111/j.1540-4781.2011.01241.x.

Riestenberg, K. J., & Manzano, R. E. C. (2019). Teaching task-based writing in Zapotec in Oaxaca, Mexico. In A. Sherris & J. K. Peyton (Eds.), *Teaching Writing to Children in Indigenous Languages: Instructional Practices from Global Contexts* (pp. 126–142). New York: Routledge.

Riestenberg, K., & Sherris, A. (2018). Task-based teaching of indigenous languages: Investment and methodological principles in Macuiltianguis Zapotec and Salish Qlispe revitalization. *Canadian Modern Language Review, 74*(3), 434–459. https://doi.org/10.3138/cmlr.4051.

Ro, E. (2018). Facilitating an L2 book club: A conversation-analytic study of task management. *The Modern Language Journal, 102*(1), 181–198. https://doi.org/10.1111/modl.12450.

Robinson, P. (2001). Task complexity, cognitive resources, and syllabus design: A triadic framework for examining task influences on SLA. In P. Robinson (Ed.), *Cognition and Second Language Instruction* (pp. 287–318). Cambridge: Cambridge University Press.

Robinson, P. (2007). Criteria for classifying and sequencing pedagogic tasks. In M. P. García Mayo (Ed.), *Investigating Tasks in Formal Language Learning* (pp. 7–26). Clevedon: Multilingual Matters.

Robinson, P. (Ed.). (2011a). *Second Language Task Complexity: Researching the Cognition Hypothesis of Language Learning and Performance.* Amsterdam: John Benjamins.

Robinson, P. (2011b). Second language task complexity, the Cognition Hypothesis, language learning, and performance. In P. Robinson (Ed.), *Second Language Task Complexity: Researching the Cognition Hypothesis of Language Learning and Performance* (pp. 3–37). Amsterdam: John Benjamins.

Robinson, P. (2015). The Cognition Hypothesis, second language task demands, and the SSARC model of pedagogic task sequencing. In M. Bygate (Ed.), *Domains and Directions in the Development of TBLT: A Decade of Plenaries from the International Conference* (pp. 87–121). Amsterdam: John Benjamins.

Robinson, P. (2022). The Cognition Hypothesis, the Triadic Componential Framework and the SSARC model. In M. J. Ahmadian & M. H. Long

(Eds.), *The Cambridge Handbook of Task-Based Language Teaching* (pp. 205–225). Cambridge: Cambridge University Press.

Samuda, V. (2001). Guiding relationships between form and meaning during task performance: The role of the teacher. In M. Bygate, P. Skehan, & M. Swain (Eds.), *Researching Pedagogic Tasks: Second Language Learning, Teaching, and Testing* (pp. 119–140). Harlow: Pearson.

Samuda, V. (2015). Tasks, design and the architecture of pedagogical spaces. In M. Bygate (Ed.), *Domains and Directions in the Development of TBLT: A Decade of Plenaries from the International Conference* (pp. 271–302). Amsterdam: John Benjamins.

Samuda, V., & Bygate, M. (2008). *Tasks in Second Language Learning.* Hampshire: Palgrave Macmillan.

Samuda, V., Bygate, M., & Van den Branden, K. (2018). Introduction: Towards a researched pedagogy for TBLT. In V. Samuda, K. Van den Branden, & M. Bygate (Eds.), *TBLT as a Researched Pedagogy* (pp. 1–22). Amsterdam: John Benjamins.

Sasayama, S., & Norris, J. (2019). Unravelling cognitive task complexity: Learning from learners' perspectives on task characteristics and second language performance. In Z. E. Wen & M. J. Ahmadian (Eds.), *Researching L2 Task Performance and Performance: In Honour of Peter Skehan* (pp. 95–132). Amsterdam: John Benjamins.

Sasayama, S., Malicka, A., & Norris, J. (in press). *Cognitive Task Complexity: A Research Synthesis and Meta-analysis.* Amsterdam: John Benjamins.

Sato, M. (2020). Metacognitive instruction for collaborative interaction: The process and product of self-regulated learning in the Chilean EFL context. In C. Lambert & R. Oliver (Eds.), *Using Tasks in Second Language Teaching: Practice in Diverse Contexts* (pp. 215–236). Bristol: Multilingual Matters.

Schmidt, R. W. (1990). The role of consciousness in second language learning. *Applied Linguistics, 11*(2), 129–158. https://doi.org/10.1093/applin/11.2.129.

Seedhouse, P. (Ed.) (2017). *Task-Based Language Learning in a Real-World Digital Environment: The European Digital Kitchen.* London: Bloomsbury.

Serafini, E. J. (2022). Adapting and advancing task-based needs analysis methodology across diverse language learning contexts. In M. J. Ahmadian & M. H. Long (Eds.), *The Cambridge Handbook of Task-Based Language Teaching* (pp. 73–98). Cambridge: Cambridge University Press.

Shehadeh, A. (2005). Task-based language learning and teaching: Theories and applications. In C. Edwards & J. Willis (Eds.), *Teachers Exploring Tasks in English Language Teaching* (pp. 13–30). London: Palgrave Macmillan.

Shehadeh, A., & Coombe, C. A. (Eds.) (2010). *Applications of Task-Based Learning in TESOL*. Alexandria, VA: TESOL.

Shehadeh, A., & Coombe, C. A. (Eds.) (2012). *Task-Based Language Teaching in Foreign Language Contexts: Research and Implementation*. Amsterdam: John Benjamins.

Sherris, A., Pete, T., Thompson, L. E., & Haynes, E. F. (2013). Task-based language teaching practices that support Salish language revitalization. In Jones, M. C. & S. Ogilvie (Eds.), *Keeping Languages Alive: Documentation, Pedagogy, and Revitalization* (pp. 155–168). Cambridge: Cambridge University Press.

Shintani, N. (2016). *Input-Based Tasks in Foreign Language Instruction for Young Learners*. Amsterdam: John Benjamins.

Skehan, P. (1996). A framework for the implementation of task-based instruction. *Applied Linguistics*, *17*(1), 38–62. https://doi.org/10.1093/applin/17.1.38.

Skehan, P. (1998). *A Cognitive Approach to Language Learning*. Oxford: Oxford University Press.

Skehan, P. (2018). *Second Language Task-Based Performance: Theory, Research, Assessment*. New York: Routledge.

Skehan, P., & Foster, P. (2012). Complexity, accuracy, fluency, and lexis in task-based performance: A synthesis of the Ealing research. In A. Housen, F. Kuiken, F., & I. Vedder (Eds.), *Dimensions of L2 Performance and Proficiency: Complexity, Accuracy, and Fluency in SLA* (pp. 199–220). Amsterdam: John Benjamins.

Solon, M., Long, A. Y., & Gurzynski-Weiss, L. (2017). Task complexity, language-related episodes, and production of L2 Spanish vowels. *Studies in Second Language Acquisition*, *39*(2), 347–380. https://doi.org/10.1017/S0272263116000425.

Spada, N. (2022). Reflecting on task-based language teaching from an Instructed SLA perspective. *Language Teaching*, *55*(1) 74–86. https://doi.org/10.1017/S0261444821000161.

Storch, N. (2002). Patterns of interaction in ESL pair work. *Language Learning*, *52*(1), 119–158. https://doi.org/10.1111/1467-9922.00179.

Tavakoli, P. (2014). Storyline complexity and syntactic complexity in writing and speaking tasks. In H. Byrnes & R. M. Manchón (Eds.), *Task-Based Language Learning – Insights from and for L2 Writing* (pp. 217–236). Amsterdam: John Benjamins.

Thai, C., & Boers, F. (2016). Repeating a monologue under increasing time pressure: Effects on fluency, complexity, and accuracy. *TESOL Quarterly*, *50*(2), 369–393. https://doi.org/10.1002/tesq.232.

Thomas, M., & Reinders, H. (Eds.). (2010). *Task-Based Language Learning and Teaching with Technology*. London: Bloomsbury.

Toker, Ş., & Sağıç, A. (2022). A task-based language needs analysis of Syrian refugee parents in Turkey. In M. J. Ahmadian & M. H. Long (Eds.), *The Cambridge Handbook of Task-Based Language Teaching* (pp. 109–120). Cambridge: Cambridge University Press.

Van de Guchte, M., Rijlaarsdam, G., Braaksma, M., & Bimmel, P. (2019). Focus . on language versus content in the pre-task: Effects of guided peer-video model observations on task performance. *Language Teaching Research*, *23*(3), 310–329. https://doi.org/10.1177/1362168817735543.

Van den Branden, K. (Ed.). (2006a). *Task-Based Language Education: From Theory to Practice*. Cambridge: Cambridge University Press.

Van den Branden, K. (2006b). Training teachers: Task-based as well? In K. Van den Branden (Ed.), *Task-Based Language Education: From Theory to Practice* (pp. 217–248). Cambridge: Cambridge University Press.

Van den Branden, K. (2015). Task-based language education: From theory to practice. . . and back again. In M. Bygate (Ed.), *Domains and Directions in the Development of TBLT: A Decade of Plenaries from the International Conference* (pp. 303–320). Amsterdam: John Benjamins.

Van den Branden, K. (2016). The role of teachers in task-based language education. *Annual Review of Applied Linguistics*, *36*, 164–181. https://doi .org/10.1017/S0267190515000070.

Van den Branden, K. (2022). *How to Teach an Additional Language: To Task or Not to Task?* Amsterdam: John Benjamins.

Van den Branden, K., & Van Gorp, K. (2021). Implementing task-based language education in primary education: Lessons learnt from the Flemish experience. *Language Teaching for Young Learners*, *3*(1), 3–27. https://doi .org/10.1075/ltyl.20013.bra.

Van den Branden, K., Van Gorp, K., & Verhelst, M. (2007). *Tasks in Action: Task-Based Language Education from a Classroom-Based Perspective*. Cambridge: Cambridge Scholars.

Vandommele, G., Van den Branden, K., & Van Gorp, K. (2018). Task-based language teaching: How task-based is it really? In V. Samuda, K. Van den Branden, & M. Bygate (Eds.), *TBLT as a Researched Pedagogy* (pp. 165–97). Amsterdam: John Benjamins.

Vasylets, O., Gilabert, R., & Manchón, R. M. (2017). The effects of mode and task complexity on second language production. *Language Learning*, *67*(2), 394–430. https://doi.org/10.1111/lang.12228.

Vieira, F. (2017). Task-based instruction for autonomy: Connections with contexts of practice, conceptions of teaching, and professional development strategies. *TESOL Quarterly, 51*(3), 693–715. https://doi.org/10.1002/tesq .384.

Weaver, C. (2012). Incorporating a formative assessment cycle into task-based language teaching in a university setting in Japan. In A. Shehadeh & C. A. Coombe (Eds.), *Task-Based Language Teaching in Foreign Language Contexts: Research and Implementation* (pp. 287–312). Amsterdam: John Benjamins.

Willis, D., & Willis, J. (2007). *Doing Task-Based Teaching.* Oxford: Oxford University Press.

Willis, J. (1996). *A Framework for Task-Based Learning.* Harlow: Longman.

Youn, S. J. (2018). Task design and validity evidence for assessment of L2 pragmatics in interaction. In N. Taguchi & Y. Kim (Eds.), *Task-Based Approaches to Teaching and Assessing Pragmatics* (pp. 217–246). Amsterdam: John Benjamins.

Yule, G. (1997). *Referential Communication Tasks.* New York: Routledge.

Zheng, X., & Borg, S. (2014). Task-based learning and teaching in China: Secondary school teachers' beliefs and practices. *Language Teaching Research, 18*(2), 205–221. https://doi.org/10.1177/1362168813505941.

Zhu, Y. (2020). Implementing tasks in young learners' language classrooms: A collaborative teacher education initiative through task evaluation. *Language Teaching Research, 26*(3), 530–551. https://doi.org/10.1177/ 1362168819894706.

Ziegler, N., & Phung, H. (2019). Technology-mediated task-based interaction: The role of modality. *ITL-International Journal of Applied Linguistics, 170*(2), 251–276. https://doi.org/10.1075/itl.19014.zie.

Acknowledgements

This Element owes its existence to a number of excellent mentors who introduced me to TBLT and encouraged my involvement, including Graham Crookes, Marta González-Lloret, John Norris, Lourdes Ortega, Teresa Pica, and Peter Robinson. Several collaborators also deserve thanks for broadening my perspective on task-based teaching and learning, including Rue Burch, Minyoung Cho, Ryo Maie, Tomoya Shirakawa, and Sakol Suethanapornkul. I would also like to acknowledge the International Association for Task-Based Language Teaching for its ongoing efforts to promote and publicize research in this area. Kanda University of International Studies has provided financial assistance for my research and I appreciate, as well, the practical insights shared by those who have joined my classes and workshops on task-based teaching. This work has benefitted greatly from the expertise of the series editors and two anonymous reviewers. Lastly, I am grateful to my father (a teacher and former education writer for the *New York Times*) for inspiring me, and to my entire family for their love and support.

Cambridge Elements ≡

Elements in Language Teaching

Heath Rose

Linacre College, University of Oxford

Heath Rose is an Associate Professor of Applied Linguistics at the University of Oxford. At Oxford, he is course director of the MSc in Applied Linguistics for Language Teaching. Before moving into academia, Heath worked as a language teacher in Australia and Japan in both school and university contexts. He is author of numerous books, such as *Introducing Global Englishes, The Japanese Writing System, Data Collection Research Methods in Applied Linguistics*, and *Global Englishes for Language Teaching*. Heath's research interests are firmly situated within the field of second language teaching, and includes work on Global Englishes, teaching English as an international language, and English Medium Instruction.

Jim McKinley

University College London

Jim McKinley is an Associate Professor of Applied Linguistics and TESOL at UCL, Institute of Education, where he serves as Academic Head of Learning and Teaching. His major research areas are second language writing in global contexts, the internationalisation of higher education, and the relationship between teaching and research. Jim has edited or authored numerous books including the *Routledge Handbook of Research Methods in Applied Linguistics, Data Collection Research Methods in Applied Linguistics*, and *Doing Research in Applied Linguistics*. He is also an editor of the journal *System*. Before moving into academia, Jim taught in a range of diverse contexts including the US, Australia, Japan, and Uganda.

Advisory Board

About the Series

This Elements series aims to close the gap between researchers and practitioners by allying research with language teaching practices, in its exploration of research informed teaching, and teaching informed research. The series builds upon a rich history of pedagogical research in its exploration of new insights within the field of language teaching.

Cambridge Elements ≡

Elements in Language Teaching

Printed in the United States
by Baker & Taylor Publisher Services